IN THE DAYS OF DRAKE

IN THE DAYS OF DRAKE

J. S. FLETCHER

WILDSIDE PRESS

IN THE DAYS OF DRAKE

Published by Wildside Press LLC.
www.wildsidebooks.com

INTRODUCTION.

In the whole history of the English people there is no period so absolutely heroic, so full of enthralling interest, as that in which the might of England made itself apparent by land and sea — the period which saw good Queen Bess mistress of English hearts and Englishmen and sovereign of the great beginnings which have come to such a magnificent fruition under Victoria. That was indeed a golden time — an age of great venture and enterprise — a period wherein men's hearts were set on personal valor and bravery — the day of great deeds and of courage most marvelous. To write down a catalogue of all the names that then were glorious, to make a list of all the daring deeds that then were done — this were an impossible task for the most painstaking of statisticians, the most conscientious of historians and chroniclers. For there were men in those days who achieved world-wide fame, such as Drake, Frobisher, Hawkins, Raleigh, Grenville, and Gilbert — but there were also other men, the rough "sea-dogs" of that time, whose names have never been remembered, or even recorded, and who were yet heroes of a quality not inferior to their commanders and leaders. All men of that age whose calling led them to adventure and enterprise could scarcely fail to find opportunity for heroism, self-denial, and sacrifice, and thus the Elizabethan Englishman of whatever station stands out to us of these later days as a great figure — the type and emblem of the England that was to be. It is this fact that makes the Elizabethan period so fascinating and so full of romance and glamour. Whenever we call it up before our mind's eye it is surrounded for us with all those qualities which go toward making a great picture. There is the awful feud

’twixt England, the modern spirit making toward progress and civilization, and Spain, the well-nigh worn-out retrogressive force that would dam the river of human thought. There is the spectacle of the Armada, baffled and beaten, and of the English war-ships under men like Drake and Frobisher, dropping like avenging angels upon some Spanish port and working havoc on the Spanish treasure galleons. There, too, are the figures of men like Grenville and Raleigh, born adventurers, leaders of men, who knew how to die as bravely and fearlessly as they had lived. And beyond all the glory and adventure there looms in the background of the picture the black cruelties of Spain, practiced in the dark corners of the earth, against which the English spirit of that day never ceased from protesting with speech and sword. It was well for the world that in that fierce contest England triumphed. Had Spain succeeded in perpetuating its hellish system, how different would life in east and west have been! But it was God’s will that not Spain but England should win — and so today we find the English-speaking peoples of the world in Great Britain and America, in Australia and Africa, free, enlightened, full of great purpose and noble aims, working out in very truth their own salvation. It is when one comes to think of this, that one first realizes the immeasurable thanks due to the heroes, known and unknown, of the Elizabethan age. Whether they stand high on the scroll of fame or lie forgotten in some quiet graveyard or in the vast oceans which they crossed, it was they, and they only, who laid the great foundations of the England and the United States of today.

J. S. FLETCHER

CHAPTER I.

OF MY HOME, FRIENDS, AND SURROUNDINGS.

Now that I am an old man, and have some leisure, which formerly I did not enjoy, I am often minded to write down my memories of that surprising and remarkable adventure of mine, which began in the year 1578, and came to an end, by God's mercy, two years later.

There are more reasons than one why I should engage in this task. Every Christmas brings a houseful of grandchildren and young folks about me, and they, though they have heard it a dozen times already, are never tired of hearing me re-tell the story which seems to them so wonderful.

Then, again, I am often visited by folk who have heard of my travels, and would fain have particulars of them from my own lips; so that ofttimes I have to tell my tale, or part of it, a dozen times in the year. Nay, upon one occasion I even told it to the King's majesty, which was when I went up to London on some tiresome law business. Sir Ralph Wood, who is my near neighbor and a Parliament man, had mentioned me to the King, and so I had to go to Whitehall and tell my story before the court, which was a hard matter for a plain-spoken country gentleman, as you may well believe.

Now all these matters have oft prompted me to write down my story, so that when any visitor of mine might ask me for it, I could satisfy him without trouble to myself, by simply putting the manuscript into his hand and bidding him read what I had there written. But until this present time I have never seemed to have opportunity such as I desired, for my duties as magistrate and church-warden have been neither light nor unimportant. Now that I have resigned them to younger hands, I have leisure time of my own, and therefore I shall now proceed to carry out the intention which has been in my mind for many years.

I was born at York, in the year 1558. My father, Richard Salkeld, was the youngest son of Oliver Salkeld, lord-of-the-manor of Beechcot-on-the-Wold, and he practiced in York as an attorney. Whether he did well or ill in this calling I know not, for at the early age of six years I was left an orphan. My father being seized by a fever, my mother devoted herself to nursing him, which was a right and proper thing to do; but the consequence was disastrous, for she also contracted the disease, and they both died, leaving me alone in the world.

However, I was not long left in this sad condition, for there presently appeared my uncle, Sir Thurstan Salkeld of Beechcot, who settled my father's affairs and took me away with him. I was somewhat afraid of him at first, for he was a good twenty years older than my father, and wore a grave, severe air. Moreover, he had been knighted by the Queen for his zealous conduct in administering the law. But I presently found him to be exceeding kind of heart, and ere many months were over I had grown fond of him, and of Beechcot. He had never married, and was not likely to, and so to the folks round about his home he now introduced me as his adopted son and heir. And thus things went very pleasantly for me, and, as children will, I soon forgot my early troubles.

I think we had nothing to cause us any vexation or sorrow at Beechcot until Dame Barbara Stapleton and her son Jasper came to share our lot. Jasper was then a lad of my own age, and like me an orphan, and the nephew of Sir Thurstan. His mother, Sir Thurstan's sister, had married Devereux Stapleton, an officer in the Queen's household, and when she was left a widow she returned to Beechcot and quartered herself and her boy on her brother. Thereafter we had trouble one way or another, for Dame Barbara could not a-bear to think that I was preferred before her own boy as Sir Thurstan's heir. Nor did she scruple to tell Sir Thurstan her thoughts on the matter, on one occasion at any rate, for I heard them talking in the great hall when they fancied themselves alone.

"'Tis neither right nor just," said Dame Barbara, "that you should make one nephew your son and heir to the exclusion of the other. What! is not Jasper as much your own flesh and blood as Humphrey?"

"You forget that Humphrey is a Salkeld in name as well as in blood," said Sir Thurstan. "If the lad's father, my poor brother Richard, had lived, he would have succeeded me as lord of Beechcot. Therefore, 'tis but right that Dick's boy should step into his father's place."

"To the hurt of my poor Jasper!" sighed Dame Barbara.

"Jasper is a Stapleton," answered Sir Thurstan. "However, sister, I will do what is right as regards your lad. I will charge myself with the cost of his education and training, and will give him a start in life, and maybe leave him a goodly sum of money when I die. Therefore, make your mind easy on that point."

But I knew, though I was then but a lad, that she would never give over fretting herself at the thought that I was to be lord of all the broad acres and wide moors of Beechcot, and that Jasper would be but a landless man. And so, though she never dare flout or oppress me in any way, for fear of Sir Thurstan's displeasure, she, without being openly unfavorable, wasted no love on me, and no doubt often wished me out of the way.

At that time Jasper and I contrived to get on very well together. We were but lads, and there was no feeling of rivalry between us. Indeed, I do not think there would ever have been rivalry between us if that foolish woman, my Aunt Barbara, had not begun sowing the seeds of discord in her son's mind. But as soon as he was old enough to understand her, she began talking to him of Beechcot and its glories, pointing out to him the wide park and noble trees, the broad acres filled with golden grain, and the great moors that stretched away for miles towards the sea; and she said, no doubt, how grand a thing it would be to be lord of so excellent an estate, and how a man might enjoy himself in its possession. Then she told him that I was to have all these things when Sir Thurstan died, and thereafter my cousin Jasper hated me. But he let his hate smoulder within him a good while before he showed it openly. One day, however, when we were out in the park with our bows, he began to talk of the matter, and after a time we got to high words.

"My mother tells me, Humphrey," said he, "that when my uncle Thurstan dies all these fair lands will pass to thee. That is not right."

"'Tis our uncle's land to do with as he pleases," I answered. "We have naught to do with it. If he likes to leave it to me, what hast thou to say in the matter? 'Tis his affair; not thine, Master Jasper. Besides, I am a Salkeld, and you are not."

"Is not my mother a Salkeld?" he asked.

"It counts not by the mother," I answered. "And, moreover, my father would have heired the estate had he lived. But be not down-hearted about it, Jasper, I will see that thou art provided for. When I am lord of Beechcot I will make thee my steward."

Now, that vexed him sore, and he flew into a violent rage, declaring that he would serve no man, and me last of all; and so violent did he become that he was foolish to look at, and thereupon I laughed at him. At that his rage did but increase, and he presently fitted an arrow to his bow and shot at me meaning, I doubt not, to put an end to me forever. But by good fortune his aim mischanced, and the arrow did no more than pin me to the tree by which I stood, passing through my clothes between the arm and the body. And at that we were both sobered, and Jasper cooled his hot temper.

"What wouldst thou have done if the arrow had passed through my heart, as it might easily have chanced to do?" I inquired of him.

"I would have gone home and told them that I had killed thee by accident," he answered readily enough. "Thou wouldst have been dead, and therefore no one could have denied my tale."

I said naught to that, but I there and then made up my mind that if ever I went shooting with him again I would keep my eyes open. For I now saw that he was not only false, but also treacherous. Indeed, I was somewhat minded to go to my uncle and tell him what had taken place between us, but I remembered that the good knight was not fond of carried tales, and therefore I refrained.

After that there was peace for some years, Dame Barbara having evidently made up her mind to take things as they were. She was mortally afraid of offending Sir Thurstan, for she had no jointure or portion of her own, and was totally dependent upon his charity for a sustenance. This made her conduct herself towards me with more consideration than I should otherwise have received from her. Possibly she thought that it might be well to keep in good favor with me in view of my succeeding Sir Thurstan at no distant period. At any rate I had no more trouble with Jasper, and I overheard no more unpleasant discussions between Dame Barbara and the knight.

From our tenth year upwards Jasper and myself daily attended the vicarage, in order to be taught Greek, Latin, and other matters by the Reverend Mr. Timotheus Herrick, vicar of Beechcot. He was a tall, thin, spindle-shanked gentleman, very absent-minded, but a great scholar. It was said of him, that if he had not married a very managing woman in the shape of Mistress Priscilla Horbury, he would never have got through the world. He had one child, Rose, of whom you will hear somewhat in this history, and she was three years younger than myself. When Jasper and I were thirteen and Rose ten years of age, she began to learn with us, and presently made such progress that she caught up to us, and then passed us, and so made us ashamed of ourselves. After that she was always in advance of us, and we used to procure her help in our lessons; then she lorded it over us, as little maidens will over big lads, and we were her humble slaves in everything.

CHAPTER II.

PHARAOH NANJULIAN.

Now it chanced that one afternoon in the June of 1575 Jasper and I were on our way from the vicarage to the manor, our lessons for that day being over. We had to pass through the village of Beechcot on our homeward journey, and it was when we were opposite the inn, then kept by Geoffrey Scales, that there occurred an incident which was to have a greater influence upon our future lives than we then imagined. In the wide space by the inn, formed by the meeting of four roads, there was gathered together a goodly company of people, who seemed to be talking as one man, and looking as with one eye at something in their midst.

"What have we here?" said Jasper, as we paused. "Is it some bear-ward with his bear, or one of those wandering Italians that go about with a guitar and a monkey?"

"I hear no music," said I. "It seems to be something of more importance than either bear or monkey. Let us see for ourselves."

So we ran forward and joined the crowd, which began presently to make way for us. Then we saw that nearly everybody in the village, saving only the men who were at work in the fields, had run together with one accord in order to stare and wonder at a man, who sat on the bench just outside the ale-house door. It was clear to me at once that he was not a native of those parts, and might possibly be a foreigner. He seemed to be of thirty-five or forty years of age, his skin and hair were very dark, and he wore a great black beard, which looked as if it had known neither comb nor scissors for many a long month. Also he was of great size and height, and on his brawny arms, which were bare from the elbows downwards, there were figures and patterns traced in blue and red, so that I at once set him down for a sailor, who had seen much life in strange countries. As for his garments, they were much stained and worn, and his feet, which were naked, were evidently callous and hardened enough to stand even the roughest roads.

When we first set eyes upon him the man was leaning back against the wall of the ale-house, looking defiantly at John Broad, the constable, who stood by him, and at Geoffrey Scales, the landlord, who stood behind Broad. In the rear, holding his chin with one hand, and looking exceeding rueful of countenance, stood Peter Pipe, the drawer. All round them hung the crowd of men and women, lads and lasses, staring open-mouthed at the great man with the black beard.

"What's all this?" said I, as we pushed our way to the front.

The sailor jumped to his feet and touched his forelock civilly enough. He looked at John Broad.

"Marry, Master Humphrey," answered John Broad, "you see this great fellow here, with a beard so long as the Turks? A' cometh into our village here, God knows where from, and must needs fall to breaking the heads of peaceable and honest men."

"'Tis a lie," said the sailor. "At least, that part of it which refers to peaceable and honest men. As to the breaking of heads, I say naught."

"But whose head hath he broken?" asked Jasper.

"Mine, sir," whined Peter Pipe. "God ha' mercy! — it sings like Benjamin Good's bees when they are hiving."

"And why did he break thy head?"

"Let him say," said the sailor. "Aye, let him say."

Peter Pipe shuffled his feet and looked out of his eye-corners. He was a creature of no spirit, and always in deadly fear of something or somebody.

"Maybe he will clout me again," said Peter.

"Fear not," said the sailor. "I would not hurt thee, thou two-penny-halfpenny drawer of small beer. Say on."

"This man, then, Master Humphrey, a' cometh into our kitchen and demands a pot of ale. So I fetched it to him and he paid me —"

"Was his money good?"

"Oh, aye, good money enough, I warrant him," said Geoffrey Scales.

"I said naught to the contrary," continued Peter. "But no sooner had he drunk than he fell to cursing me for a thief, and swore that I had served him with small beer, and with that he caught up the tankard and heaved it at me with such force that my jaw is well-nigh broken."

"And didst serve him with small beer?"

"I serve him with small beer! Nay, Master Humphrey, bethink you. As if I did not know the difference betwixt small beer and good ale!"

"That thou dost not," said the sailor. "Young sir, listen to me. I know thee not, and I fear thee not, and I know not why I should trouble to talk to thee. But thou seemest to be in authority."

"'Tis Sir Thurstan's nephew," whispered the constable.

"What know I of Sir Thurstan? Young sir, I am a man of Cornwall, and my name it is Pharaoh Nanjulian. They know me in Marazion. I have been on a venture to the North Seas — plague take it, there is naught but ice and snow there, with white bears twenty feet long —"

"List to him!" said someone in the crowd.

"I will show thee the white bear's trick, an' thou doubtest me. But to proceed. Young sir, we were wrecked — sixteen good men and true we were — off the Norroway coasts, which methinks are fashioned of iron, and we underwent trials, yea, and hunger. After a time we came to Drontheim —"

"Where is that?"

"A sea-coast town of Norroway, young sir. And thence we took ship to Scarborough. But there was no ship at Scarborough going south, wherefore I set out for mine own country on foot. And today, which is my first on this journey, I came to this inn for a pint of good ale, and paid my money for it too, whereupon yonder scurvy knave gives me small beer, thin as water. And I, being somewhat hot and choleric of temper, threw the measure at him, and rewarded him for his insolence. So now I will go on my way, for 'tis a brave step from here to Marazion, and I love not ye north-country folk."

"Not so fast," quoth John Broad. "Thou must needs see Sir Thurstan before we let thee go."

"What want I with Sir Thurstan?"

"Marry, naught; but he may want something with thee. We allow not that wandering rascals shall break the peace in our village."

"If thou talkest to me like that, Master Constable, I shall break thy head, and in such a fashion that thou wilt never more know what peace is. We men of Devon and Cornwall allow no man to lord it over us."

"Thou shalt to Sir Thurstan, anyhow," said John Broad. "We will see what the law says to thee. I fear me thou art a man of lawless behavior; and, moreover, there are strange characters about at this moment."

"Dame Good had two fowls stolen last night," said a voice in the crowd.

"Yea, and there are two fine linen sheets stolen from the vicarage hedge," piped another.

"He looks a strange mortal," said a third.

"And wears gold rings in his ears," cried a fourth. "A' must be a foreigner, and maybe a Papist."

"Foreigner or Papist I am not, good folks, but a true-born Englishman, and a good hater of all Frenchmen and Spaniards. So let me go forward peaceably. As for the clout I gave Master Peter, here is a groat to mend it. I have but a round dozen, or I would give him two."

With that he would have moved forward, but John Broad barred the way.

"Not till I have taken thee before his worship," said he. "What, am I not constable of this parish, and duly sworn to arrest all suspicious persons, sturdy beggars, and what not?"

The sailor paused and drew his breath, and looked at the constable's round figure as if in doubt what to do.

"I am loth to hurt thee," said he, "but if I hit thee, Master Constable, thou wilt never more drink ale nor smell beef. Know that once in Palermo there came upon me a great brown bear that had got loose from his ward, and I hit him fair and square between the eyes, and he fell, and when they took him up, his skull it was cracked. Is thy skull harder than the bear's?"

At this John Broad trembled and shrank away, but continued to mutter something about the law and its majesty.

"You had better go with him before my uncle," said I. "He will deal justly with thee. He is hard upon no man, but it might fare ill with John Broad if Sir Thurstan knew that he had suffered you to go unapprehended."

"Oh, if you put it in that way," he answered, and turned again, "I will go with you. Heaven send that the good gentleman do not detain me, for I would fain reach York tonight."

So we all moved off to the manor, and as many as could find room crowded into the great hall where Sir Thurstan sat to deliver judgment on all naughty and evilly-disposed persons. And presently he came and took his seat in the justice-chair and commanded silence, and bade John Broad state his case. Then Peter Pipe gave his testimony, and likewise Geoffrey Scales, and then Sir Thurstan called upon the sailor to have his say, for he made a practice of never condemning any man unheard.

After he had heard them all, my uncle considered matters for a moment and then delivered judgment, during which everybody preserved strict silence.

"I find, first of all," said he, "that Peter Pipe, the drawer, did serve this man with small beer instead of good ale. For what! I watched the man as he told his story, and he did not lie."

"I thank your honor," said the sailor.

"Wherefore I recommend Geoffrey Scales to admonish Peter at his convenience —"

"Yea, and with a stick, your honor," said Geoffrey.

"So that he transgress not again. Nevertheless, the sailor did wrong to maltreat Peter. There is law to be had, and no man should administer his own justice. Wherefore I fine thee, sailor, and order thee to pay ten groats to the court."

"As your honor wills," said the man, and handed over the money. "I have now one left to see me all the way to Marazion. But justice is justice."

"Clear my hall, John Broad," said my uncle. This order the constable carried out with promptitude. But when the sailor would have gone, Sir Thurstan bade him stay, and presently he called him to his side and held converse with him.

"Dost thou propose to walk to Marazion?" he asked.

"With God's help, sir," answered the man.

"Why not try Hull? Thou mightest find a ship there for a southern port."

"I had never thought of it, your honor. How far away may Hull be?"

"Forty miles. What means hast thou?"

"But one groat, sir. But then I have become used to hardships."

"Try Hull: thou wilt find a ship there, I doubt not. Hold, here are twelve shillings for thee. Humphrey, have him to the kitchen and give him a good meal ere he starts."

"Your honor," said the sailor, "is a father and a brother to me. I shall not forget."

"Do thy duty," said Sir Thurstan.

So I took the man to the kitchen, and fed him, and soon he went away.

"Young master," said he, "if I can ever repay this kindness I will, yea, with interest. Pharaoh Nanjulian never forgets."

With that he went away, and we saw him no more.

CHAPTER III.

ROSE.

There being no disposition on my part to renew our differences, and none on his to lead up to an open rupture, my cousin Jasper Stapleton and I got on together very well, until we had reached the age of nineteen years, when a new and far more important matter of contention arose between us.

Now, our first quarrel had arisen over the ultimate disposition of my uncle's estates; our second was as to which should be lord over the heart and hand of a fair maiden. To both of us the second quarrel was far more serious than the first — which is a thing that will readily be understood by all young folks. It seemed to both of us that not all the broad acres of Beechcot, nay, of Yorkshire itself, were to be reckoned in comparison with the little hand of Mistress Rose Herrick.

For by that time Mistress Rose had grown to be a fair and gracious maiden, whose golden hair, floating from under her dainty cap, was a dangerous snare for any hot-hearted lad's thoughts to fall entangled in. So sweet and gracious was she, so delightful her conversation, so bewitching her eyes, that I marvel not even at this stretch of time that I then became her captive and slave for life. Nor do I marvel, either, that Jasper Stapleton was equally enslaved by her charms. It had indeed been wonderful if he or I had made any resistance to them.

As to myself, the little blind god pierced my heart with his arrow at a very early stage. Indeed, I do not remember any period of my life when I did not love Rose Herrick more dearly than anything else in God's fair world. To me she was all that is sweet and desirable, a companion whose company must needs make the path of life a primrose path; and, therefore, even when I was a lad, I looked forward to the time when I might take her hand in mine, and enter with her upon the highway which all of us must travel.

However, when I was come to nineteen years of age, being then a tall and strapping lad, and somewhat grave withal, it came to my mind that I should find out for myself what feelings Rose had with regard to me, and therefore I began to seek her company, and to engage her in more constant conversation than we had hitherto enjoyed. And the effect of this was that my love for her, which had until then been of a placid nature, now became restless and unsatisfied, and longed to know whether it was to be answered with love or finally dismissed.

Thus I became somewhat moody and taciturn, and took to wandering about the land by myself, by day or night, so that Sir Thurstan more than once asked me if I had turned poet or fallen in love. Now, both these things were true, for because I had fallen in love I had also turned poet; as, I suppose, every lover must. In sooth, I had scribbled lines and couplets, and here and there a song, to my sweet mistress, though I had never as yet mustered sufficient courage to show her what I had written. That, I think, is the way with all lovers who make rhymes. There is a satisfaction to them in the mere writing of them; and I doubt not that they often read over their verses, and in the reading find a certain keen and peculiar sort of pleasure which is not altogether unmixed with pain.

Now it chanced that one day in the early spring of 1578 I had been wandering about the park of Beechcot, thinking of my passion and its object, and my thoughts as usual had clothed themselves in verses. Wherefore, when I again reached the house, I went into the library and wrote down my rhymes on paper, in order that I might put them away with my other compositions. I will write them down here from the copy I then made. It lies before me now, a yellow, time-stained sheet, and somehow it brings back to me the long-dead days of happiness which came before my wonderful adventure.

TO ROSE.

When I first beheld thee, dear,
Day across the land was breaking,
April skies were fine and clear
And the world to life was waking;
All was fair
In earth and air:
Spring lay lurking in the sedges:
SuddenlyI looked on thee
And straight forgot the budding hedges.

When I first beheld thee, sweet,
Madcap Love came gayly flying
Where the woods and meadows meet:
Then I straightway fell a-sighing.
Fair, I said,
Are hills and glade
And sweet the light with which they're laden,
But ah, to me,
Nor flower nor tree
Are half so sweet as yonder maiden.

Thus when I beheld thee, love,
Vanished quick my first devotion,
Earth below and heaven above
And the mystic, magic ocean

Seemed to me
No more to be.
I had eyes for naught but thee, dear,
With his dart
Love pierced my heart
And thou wert all in all to me, dear!

Now, as I came to an end of writing these verses I was suddenly aware of someone standing at my side, and when I looked up, with anger and resentment that anyone should spy upon my actions, I saw my cousin Jasper at my elbow, staring at the two words, "To Rose," which headed my composition. I sprang to my feet and faced him.

"That is like you, cousin," said I, striving to master my anger, "to act the spy upon a man."

"As you please," he answered. "I care what no man thinks of my actions. But there," pointing to the paper, "is proof of what I have long suspected. Humphrey, you are in love with Mistress Rose Herrick!"

"What if I am?" said I.

"Nothing, but that I also am in love with her, and mean to win her," he replied.

After that there was silence.

"We cannot both have her," said I at last.

"True," said he. "She shall be mine."

"Not if I can prevent it, cousin. At any rate she has the principal say in this matter."

"Thou hast not spoken to her, Humphrey?"

"What is that to thee, cousin? But I have not."

"Humphrey, thou wilt heir our uncle's lands. Thou hast robbed me of my share in them. I will not be robbed of my love. Pish! do not stay me. Thou art hot-tempered and boyish, but I am cold as an icicle. It is men like me whose love is deep and determined, and therefore I swear thou shalt not come between me and Rose Herrick."

I watched him closely, and saw that he valued nothing of land or money as he valued his passion, and that he would stay at nothing in order to gain his own ends. But I was equally firm.

"What do you propose, Jasper?" I asked. "It is for Mistress Rose Herrick to decide. We cannot both address her at the same time."

"True," he said; "true. I agree that you have the same right to speak to her that I have. Let us draw lots. The successful one shall have the first chance. Do you agree?"

I agreed willingly, because I felt certain that even if Jasper beat me he would have no chance with Rose. There was something in my heart that told me she would look on me, and on me only, with favor.

We went out into the stackyard, and agreed that each of us should draw a straw from a wheat-stack. He that drew the longest straw should have the first right of speaking. Then we put our hands to the stack and drew our straws. I beat him there — my straw was a good foot longer than his.

"You have beaten me again," he said. "Is it always to be so? But I will wait, cousin Humphrey."

And so he turned away and left me.

Now, seeing how matters stood, it came to my mind that I had best put my fortune to the test as quickly as possible, and therefore I made haste over to the vicarage in order to find Rose and ask her to make me either happy or miserable. And as good luck would have it, I found her alone in the vicarage garden, looking so sweet and gracious that I was suddenly struck dumb, and in my confusion could think of naught but that my face was red, my attire negligent, and my whole appearance not at all like that of a lover.

"Humphrey," said Rose, laughing at me, "you look as you used to look in the days when you came late to your lessons, from robbing an orchard or chasing Farmer Good's cattle, or following the hounds. Are you a boy again?"

But there she stopped, for I think she saw something in my eyes that astonished her. And after that I know not what we said or did, save that presently we understood one another, and for the space of an hour entirely forgot that there were other people in the world, or, indeed, that there was any world at all.

So that evening I went home happy. And as I marched up to the manor, whistling and singing, I met my cousin. He looked at me for a moment, and then turned on his heel.

"I see how it is," he said. "You have no need to speak."

"Congratulate me, at any rate, cousin," I cried.

"Time enough for that," said he.

And from that moment he hated me, and waited his opportunity to do me a mischief.

CHAPTER IV.

FOUL PLAY.

When a man has conceived a deadly hatred of one of his fellow-men, and has further resolved to let slip no chance of satisfying it, his revenge becomes to him simply a question of time, for the chance is sure to come sooner or later.

It was this conviction, I think, that kept my cousin Jasper Stapleton quiet during the next few months. He knew that in due course his revenge would have an opportunity of glutting itself, and for that evil time he was well content to wait. You may wonder that so young a man should have possessed such cruel feelings toward one who had never done him any willful wrong. But as events proved Jasper was of an exceeding cruel and malignant nature, and his wickedness was all the worse because it was of a cold and calculating sort. If a man gave him an honest straightforward blow or buffet, it was not Jasper's way to strike back there and then, face to face, but rather to wait until some evil chance presented itself — and then, his adversary's back being turned, Jasper would plant a dagger between his shoulders. In other words, he bided his time, and when he did strike, struck at an unguarded place.

Now at that time I had very little idea that Jasper entertained such hard thoughts of me — my knowledge of his cruelty only came by later experience. All that spring and summer of 1578 I was living in a very paradise, and cared not for Jasper or Dame Barbara or anybody else. My uncle had sanctioned the betrothal of Rose Herrick and myself, and the good vicar had given us his blessing in choice Latin. There had been some little scolding of us from both manor-house and vicarage, for Sir Thurstan and Master Timotheus both thought us too young to talk of love and marriage; but in the end our pleadings prevailed, and it was arranged that we were to consider ourselves plighted lovers, and that our wedding was to take place in two years. This settled, there was naught but happiness for me and Rose. I think we spent most of that summer out of doors, wandering about the Chase, and talking as lovers will, of all the days to come. Never once did there come a cloud over the fair heaven of our hopes, unless it was once, when in a remote corner of the woods, we suddenly came face to face with Jasper Stapleton. He had been out with his bow, and when we met him he was advancing along the path, with a young deer slung over his shoulders. At the sound of our footsteps on the crackling underwood, he stopped, looked up, and, recognizing us, turned hastily away and vanished in the thick bushes.

"Why did Jasper go away so suddenly?" asked Rose.

"Because he was not minded to meet us," said I.

"But why? And I have not seen him these many weeks — he seems to avoid me. Did you mark his face, Humphrey, — how white it turned when he set eyes on us? And there was a look on it that frightened me — a look that seemed to promise no love for you, Humphrey," she said.

"Have no fear, sweetheart," I answered. "Jasper is a strange fellow, but he will do me no harm. He is only disappointed because I have won a flower that he would fain have possessed himself."

"What do you mean?" she asked.

"I mean, sweetheart, that Jasper was much in love with Mistress Rose Herrick, and liked not that Humphrey Salkeld should win her. There — perhaps I have done wrong to tell thee this; but, indeed, I like not mysteries."

But so strange are women, that Rose immediately fell to sighing and lamenting on Jasper's woes. "It is sad," she said, "that any man should sorrow over a maiden's pretty face, when there are so many girls in the world." This train of thought, however, suddenly slipped from her when she remembered Master Jasper's ugly looks.

"He will do you a mischief, Humphrey," she said. "I saw it in his eyes. He hates you. They say that jealousy breeds murder — oh! what if Jasper should try to kill you?"

I laughed at the notion. I was so cock-a-whoop at that time, so elated with my love and my fair prospects, that I did not believe anything could harm me, and said so. Nevertheless, I believe Rose was from that time much concerned as to the relations between me and Jasper, having some woman-born notion that all might not go so well as I, in my boyish confidence, anticipated. But when she set forth her fears from time to time, I only laughed at her, never thinking that my cousin's opportunity was already close at hand.

Early in the month of October in that year Sir Thurstan called Jasper and myself into the library one morning, and informed us that he had business for us at the port of Scarborough. There was, he said, a ship coming over from Hamburg, the master of which had been entrusted with a certain commission from him, and as the vessel was now due, he wished us to go over to Scarborough and complete the matter, by receiving certain goods and paying the master his money. Neither Jasper nor I were displeased at the notion of this trip, for we were both minded to see a little of the world. True, I did not like the idea of being separated from my sweetheart for several days; but then, as she said, there would be the delight of looking forward to our meeting again. Alas! neither of us knew that that meeting was not to take place for three long and weary years.

We set out from Beechcot, Jasper and I, one Monday morning, having with us money wherewith to pay the charges of the ship-master. From the manor-house to Scarborough there was a distance of twenty odd miles, and therefore we rode our horses. Sir Thurstan had given us instructions to put up at the Mermaid Tavern, near the harbor, and there we accordingly stabled our beasts and made arrangements for our own accommodation. The ship which we were expecting had not yet arrived, and was not likely to come in before the next day, so that we had naught to do but look about us and derive what amusement we could from the sights of the little fishing town. Small as the place was, it being then little more than a great cluster of houses nestling under the shadow of the high rock on which stands Scarborough Castle, it was still a place of importance to us, who had never for many years seen any town or village bigger than our own hamlet of Beechcot, where there were no more than a dozen farmsteads and cottages all told. Also the sailors, who hung about the harbor or on the quay-side, or who sat in their boats mending their nets and spinning their yarns one to another, were sources of much interest, so that we felt two or three days of life in their company would not be dull nor misspent. Moreover, the merchant, whose ship it was that carried Sir Thurstan's goods, showed us much attention, and would have us to his house to talk with him and tell him of our uncle, whose acquaintance he had made many years previously, but had not been able to cultivate.

There is, near the harbor of Scarborough, lying half-hid amongst the narrow streets which run up towards the Castle Hill, a quaint and curious inn known as the Three Jolly Mariners. At its door stands a figure carved in wood, which at some time, no doubt, acted as figure-head to a ship, but whether it represents Venus or Diana, Hebe or Minerva, I do not know. Inside, the house more resembles the cabin of a vessel than the parlor of a tavern. On the walls are many curious things brought by mariners from foreign parts, together with relics of ships that had made many voyages from the harbor outside, and had finally come home to be broken up. In this place, half-parlor, half-cabin, there assembled men of seafaring life: salts, young and old, English, Scotch, Norwegians, and Danes, with now and then a Frenchman or Spaniard, so that there is never any lack of interesting and ofttimes marvelous discourse.

Our ship not having come in on the Tuesday night, Jasper and I, in company with the merchant aforesaid, entered the Three Jolly Mariners, and having saluted the assembled company, sat down to wait awhile, the harbor-master thinking it likely that our vessel would shortly be signaled. There were several men in the inn, drinking and talking, and all were of interest in my eyes, but one of them much more so than the others. He was a stoutly-built, tall man of middle age, dressed in what seemed to my eyes a very fantastic style, there being more color in his dress than was then usual. He had a high, white fore-head, over which his jet-black hair was closely cropped, his eyes were set rather too near together to be pleasant, his nose was long, his teeth very white and large, and his beard, almost as black as his hair, was trimmed to a point. As he sat and listened to the conversation around him he never laughed, but occasionally he smiled, exposing his cruel teeth, and reminding me of a dog that shows its fangs threateningly.

Our friend the merchant whispered to us that this gentleman was a certain Captain Manuel Nunez, who came trading to Scarborough from Seville. He further informed us that his ship now lay outside in the harbor, and was a fine vessel, of very graceful proportions, and much more beautiful to look at than our English ships, which are somewhat squat and ugly, though not difficult to handle.

"And although he is a Spaniard," continued our friend, "this Senor Nunez is well liked here, for he makes himself courtly and agreeable to those who have to do with him, so that our recent relations with his country have not prevented him from coming amongst us."

However, there was something about the man which almost made me afraid. He reminded me of a viper which I once killed in Beechcot Woods. And though we entered into conversation with him that night, and found him a mightily agreeable companion, I still preserved the notion that he was a man not to be trusted, and like to prove cruel and treacherous.

The following day, going down to the harbor-wall to see if there were any signs of our ship, I saw my cousin engaged in close conversation with Senor Nunez. I did not intrude myself upon them, but presently the Spaniard, catching sight of me, came to my side, and with a courteous salutation addressed me.

"I have been inviting your good cousin, Master Stapleton, to go aboard my vessel yonder," said he, "and I would tender the same courtesy to yourself, Master Salkeld. It is not often that an English country gentleman has a chance of seeing a Spanish ship in these sad days, unless, alack! it be in this deplorable warfare; and, therefore, I thought you might both be glad of this opportunity."

"What do you say, Humphrey?" asked Jasper, who had now approached us. "I would like to see the inside of a Spanish ship. If 'tis aught like the outside it should be well worth an examination."

"A look at the Santa Luisa will repay your trouble, gentlemen," said the Spaniard with a proud smile. "There is no faster ship for her size on the high seas."

"I am agreeable," said I. "Our own ship is not yet come, and time begins to hang heavy."

"Then you shall come on board tonight," said Captain Nunez. "Until six of the clock I am engaged on shore, but at that hour I will have a boat awaiting us at the harbor stairs, and you shall go aboard with me, gentlemen."

So we agreed and parted with him, Jasper full of the matter, and exclaiming that we should have much to tell the folks at home. I, however, was beginning to get somewhat impatient with respect to our own ship, which its owner now believed to have been unexpectedly detained, and I only regarded the visit to the Santa Luisa as a diversion.

At six o'clock that night, Jasper and I met the Spaniard at the harbor stairs and went on board his vessel. We found the Santa Luisa to be a very fine ship, and of much more pretentious appearance as regarded her fittings than our own English trading vessels. We passed an hour or so in examining her, and were then pressed by Senor Nunez to enter his cabin and enjoy his hospitality.

I have no very clear recollection of what followed. I remember that we ate and drank, that the Spaniard was vastly amusing in his discourse, and that I began to feel mighty sleepy. After that I must have gone to sleep.

When I came to my full senses again I was lying in a hammock, and I could tell from the motion of the ship that we were at sea in a good, fresh wind. The Spaniard stood by me, regarding me attentively. I started up and addressed him.

"Senor Nunez! I have been asleep. Where am I? The ship seems to be moving!"

"The ship is moving, Master Salkeld," he answered, in his smooth, rich voice. "At this moment she is off the Lincolnshire coast. You have slept for twelve hours."

CHAPTER V.

PHARAOH NANJULIAN AGAIN.

I do not know to this day how I got out of the hammock, but no sooner did I hear the Spanish captain utter these words than I made haste to go on deck and examine the truth of his statement for myself. But before I could reach the companion I reeled and staggered, and should have fallen, if Nunez had not seized my arm and supported me. He helped me to a seat, and handed me a glass containing a restorative.

"You are not well," he said. "But you will come round presently."

"Senor!" I cried, "what is the meaning of this? Why am I on this ship, and why are we at sea? How is it that I am not at Scarborough? There has been some treachery — some foul play!"

"Nay," said he, "be moderate, I entreat you, Senor. Do not let there be any talk of treachery. Am I not serving you as a friend?"

"I do not comprehend anything of what you say," I answered. "There is some mystery here. Again I ask you — why am I on board your ship and at sea?"

"And I ask you, Senor, where else did you expect to be but on board my ship and at sea?"

I stared at the man in amaze and wonder. He returned my gaze unflinchingly, but I felt certain that in his eyes there was a cruel mockery of me, and my blood seemed to turn cold within me as I recognized that I was in the Spaniard's power. But, being now in a desperate mood, I strove to be cool and to keep my wits about me.

"I expected to be at Scarborough, Senor," I said. "Where else? I remember coming aboard your vessel and eating and drinking with you, but after that I must have fallen asleep. I wake and find myself at sea."

"Naturally you do," said he with a smile. "Allow me, Master Salkeld, to recall to you certain incidents which took place last night. You came on board my ship with your cousin, Master Stapleton, and I offered you my poor hospitality. Was that all that took place?"

"It was," said I, confidently enough.

"That is strange," said he, giving me another of his queer looks. "I fear you have undergone some strange mental change in your long sleep. But as I perceive that you do not understand me, I will explain matters to you. Last night, Master Salkeld, as you and your cousin sat at meat with me, you explained to me that you had committed some great crime against the laws of your country, and that it was necessary, if you would save your head, to leave England at once. I remarked that I was about to set sail for the West Indies, and should be pleased to take you as my passenger, whereupon you and your cousin having consulted together, you paid me the passage-money — and here we are."

The man told me all this with the utmost assurance, his face utterly unmoved and his strange eyes inscrutable. It was a lie from beginning to end, and I knew it to be a lie. Nevertheless, I knew also that I was powerless, and I made up my mind to act prudently.

"Senor," I replied, "as between you and me, I may as well tell you that I do not believe a single word of what you have said. There has been treachery — and it lies with you and my rascal cousin, Jasper Stapleton. I have committed no crime against the laws, and I wish to be put ashore at your earliest opportunity."

"You shall be obeyed, Master Salkeld," he replied, bowing low, but with a mocking smile about his lips.

"Where do you first touch land?" I inquired.

"I have already told you, Master Salkeld. Somewhere in the West Indies."

"But you do not mean to carry me to the West Indies?" I cried. "Why, 'tis a journey of many thousands of miles!"

"Precisely. Nevertheless, you must undertake it. We touch no land until we make Barbadoes or Martinique."

I said no more; it was useless. I was in the man's power. Nothing that I could say or do would alter his purpose. There had been villainy and treachery — and my cousin, Jasper Stapleton, had worked it. I comprehended everything at that moment. I had been lured on board the Spanish vessel and subsequently drugged, in order that Jasper might rid himself of my presence. That was plainly to be seen. But what of the future? The West Indies, I knew, were thousands of miles away. They were in the hands of our hereditary enemies, the Spaniards. From them I should receive scant mercy or consideration. I was penniless — for my money had disappeared — and even if I had possessed money, what would it have benefited me in a savage land like that to which I was being carried? I might wait there many a long year without meeting with an English ship. I turned to the Spaniard.

"So I am a prisoner, Senor, — your prisoner?"

"My ship and my goods are at your disposal, Senor," he replied.

"So long as I do not make any demands upon them, eh?"

"Say unreasonable demands, Master Salkeld. As a matter of fact you are free to walk or stand, sit or lie, wake or sleep as you please. I entertain you as I best can until we touch land — and then you go your own way. You have made a contract with me, you have paid your money, and now I have nothing to do but carry out my share of the bargain."

"And that is — ?"

"To take you to the West Indies."

"Very good, Senor. Now we understand each other. You will perhaps not object to my telling you, that when I next meet my cousin, Master Jasper Stapleton, I will break his head for his share in this foul conspiracy."

"I do not object in the least, Master Salkeld. But you do well to say, when you next meet him."

"Why so, Senor?"

"Because it is so highly improbable. Indeed, you will never be so near England again as you are at this moment."

I looked through the port, and saw the long, flat Lincolnshire coast. The day was dull and heavy, and the land was little more than a gray bank, but it meant much to me. I was being carried away from all that I loved, from my sweetheart, my uncle, my friends, from everything that had grown a part of my daily life. And I was going — where? That I knew not. Not to the West Indies — no, I was sure of that. Captain Manuel Nunez was an accomplished liar in everything, and I felt sure that he had another lie in reserve yet. At the thought of him and of Jasper's villainy the blood boiled in my veins, and tears of rage and despair gathered in my eyes. But what was the use of anger or sorrow? I was powerless.

I now made up my mind to show a good face to all these troubles and difficulties, and, therefore, I strove to be as much at my ease as was possible under the circumstances. I walked the decks, talked with such of the men as knew a word or two of English, and cultivated as much of the captain's acquaintance as my aversion to his wickedness would permit. I learnt the names of masts, sheets, stays, and sprits, and picked up other information of seafaring matters, thinking that it might some day be useful to me. I am bound to say that Senor Manuel Nunez was very courteous towards me. But what avails courtesy, when the courteous man is only waiting his time to injure you?

We had been at sea something like three weeks, and had passed Ushant four days previously, when, sailing south-by-west, we were overtaken by a gale and had to run before it with bare poles. Upon the second morning, our lookout, gazing across a stormy sea, cried that he saw a man clinging to a piece of wreckage on the lee bow, and presently all those on deck were conscious of the same sight. The man was drifting and tossing half a mile away, and had seen us, for he was making frantic efforts to attract our notice. I was somewhat surprised when Captain Nunez took steps to rescue him, for it would have fitted in with my notion of his character if he had suffered the wretch to remain unaided, However, he sent off a boat, which eventually brought away the man from his piece of wreckage, and had hard work to make the ship again, for the sea was running hard and high. The rescued man crouched in the stern, hiding his head in his hands, so that I did not see his face until he came aboard. Then it seemed familiar, but I could not bethink me where I had seen it before.

"And who art thou, friend?" asked Nunez.

"A mariner of Plymouth, good sir," answered the man, "and sole survivor of the ship Hawthorn. Lost she is, and all hands, save only me."

Then I suddenly recognized him. It was the Cornish sailor, Pharaoh Nanjulian. So the sea had given me a friend in need.

CHAPTER VI.

SCHEMES AND STRATAGEMS.

I was not minded to let Captain Nunez and the crew — every man of which was either Spaniard or Portugee — see that I had any knowledge of the man whom they had rescued, and therefore I presently went below and kept out of the way for a while. Somehow I felt a considerable sense of gratification at the thought of the Cornishman's presence on board. He seemed to me a man of resource and of courage, and I no sooner set eyes on him in this remarkable fashion, than I began to think how he might aid me in making my escape from my present position.

After a time Nunez came down into the cabin where I sat, and began to talk with me.

"We have fallen in with a countryman of yours, Master Salkeld," said he, regarding me closely, as if he wished to see how I took the news.

"Indeed!" said I. "The man just come aboard?"

"The same. A native of Cornwall, with an outlandish name, and an appetite as large as his body, judging by the way he eats."

"He is no doubt hungry, Senor," I said. "Perhaps he has been tossing about for a while."

"A day and a night. One additional mouth, Master Salkeld, is what I did not bargain for."

"But you would not have allowed the man to drift away to starvation and death?" I said.

"His life was no concern of mine, Master Salkeld. But I can make him useful; therefore he was worth saving. I shall enroll him as one of my crew, and carry him to the Indies."

"And then?"

"Then he will go ashore with you, unless he prefers to go back with me to Cadiz — which he probably will not do."

He left me then, and I sat wondering what he meant by saying that the English sailor would probably not care to go back to Spain with him. There seemed something sinister in his meaning. But I gave over thinking about it, for I was by that time firmly convinced that Captain Manuel Nunez was a thorough-paced scoundrel, and well fitted to undertake all manner of villainy, despite his polished manners and fine words. Also, I was certain that there was in store for me some unpleasant and possibly terrible fate, which I was powerless to avoid and which was certain to come. Therefore I had resigned myself to my conditions, and only hoped to show myself a true Englishman when my time of trouble came.

Nevertheless, many a sad hour and day did I spend, looking across the great wild waste of gray water and wondering what they were doing at Beechcot. In my sad thoughts and in my dreams I could see the little hamlet nestling against the purple Wold; the brown leaves piled high about the shivering hedgerows; the autumn sunlight shining over the close-cropped fields; and in the manor-house the good knight, my uncle, seated by his wood-fire, wondering what had become of me. Also I could see the old vicarage and the vicar, good Master Timotheus, thumbing his well-loved folios, and occasionally pushing his spectacles from his nose to look round and inquire whether there was yet news of the boy Humphrey. But more than these, I saw my sweetheart's face, sad and weary with fear, and her eyes seemed as if they looked for something and were unsatisfied. And then would come worse thoughts — thoughts of Jasper and his villainy, and of what it might have prompted him to in the way of lies. He would carry home a straight and an ingenious tale — I was very sure of that. He would tell them I was drowned or kidnaped, and nobody would doubt his story. That was the worst thought of all — that my dear ones should be thinking of me as one dead while I was simply a prisoner, being carried I knew not where, nor to what fate.

On the evening of the second day after the Cornish sailor came aboard, the weather having moderated and the ship making good progress, I was leaning over the port bulwarks moodily gazing at the sea, when I felt a touch on my hand. Looking round, I saw the Englishman engaged in coiling a rope close to me. He continued his task and spoke in a low voice.

"I recognized you, master," said he. "I looked through the skylight last night as you talked with the captain, and I knew you again. I know not how you came here, nor why, but it is strange company for a young English gentleman."

"I was trapped on board," I said.

"I thought so," he responded. "But speak low, master, and take no heed of me. We can converse while I work, but it will not do for us to be seen talking too much. The less we are noticed together the better for our necks. How came you here, master? I had no thought of seeing you in such company."

I told him as briefly as possible while he continued to coil the rope.

"Aye," said he, when I had finished my story, "I expected something of that sort. Well, I am glad that the old Hawthorn left me swimming, though sorry enough that all her merry men are gone down below. But what! death must come. Now, young master, what can we do? I swore a solemn oath when your good uncle befriended me that I would serve you. This is the time. What can I do?"

"Alas," said I, "I know not."

"Do you know whither we are bound?" he asked.

"The Captain says to the West Indies. But I do not know if that be true or false."

"More likely to be false than true, master. Now, then, hearken to me, young sir. I have seen a deal of life, and have been a mariner this thirty year or more. We must use our wits. Can you, do you think, find out what our destination really is?"

"I am afraid not," I replied. "Nunez will not tell me more than he has already told me."

"True," said he; "true — you will get naught out of him. But I have a better chance. I can talk to the men — well it is that I know their lingo sufficiently for that. But nay, I will not talk to them, I will listen instead. They do not know that I understand Spanish. There are three of them speak broken English — they shall do the talking. I will keep my ears open for their Spanish — peradventure I shall hear something worth my trouble. You see, master, if we only know where we are going, and what we have to expect when we get there, we shall be in a much better position than we are now. For now we are as men that walk in a fog, not knowing where the next step will take them."

"I will do whatever you wish," said I.

"Then be careful not to have over-much converse with me, master. Yon Nunez has the eye of a hawk and the stealth of a viper, and if he does but suspect that you and

I are in treaty together, he will throw me overboard with a dagger wound under my shoulder-blade."

"How shall we hold converse, then?"

"As we are now doing. If I have aught to tell you I will give you a sign when you are near me. A wink, or a nod, or a cough — either will do. And what I have to say I will say quickly, so that whoever watches us will think we do no more than pass the time of day."

So for that time we parted, and during the next few days I watched for Pharaoh Nanjulian's sign eagerly, and was sadly disappointed when I received it not. Indeed, for nearly a week he took no notice of me whatever, giving me not even a sign of recognition as I passed him on the deck, so that Nunez was minded to remark upon his indifference.

"Your countryman seems but a surly dog," said he. "I should have thought he would have sought your company, Master Salkeld, but he seems to care no more for it than for that of the ship's dog."

"He is a Cornishman and a sailor, and I am a Yorkshireman and a gentleman," said I. "In England we should not associate one with the other, so wherefore should we here?"

"Nay, true, unless that you are companions in adversity, and that makes strange bedfellows," said he. "But you English are not given to talking."

I hoped that he really thought so, and that he had no idea of the thoughts within me. I was ready enough to talk when Pharaoh Nanjulian gave the signal.

It came at last as he stood at the wheel one night, and I stood near, apparently idling away my time.

"Now, master," said he, "continue looking over the side and I will talk. I have found out where we are going."

"Well?" I said, eager enough for his news.

"We are bound for Vera Cruz, master."

"Where is that? In the West Indies?"

"It is a port of Mexico, master, and in the possession of the Spaniards, who are devils in human shape."

"And what will they do with us there?"

"That I have also found out. It seems that your good cousin, Master Stapleton, did make a bargain with this noble Spanish gentleman, Captain Nunez, for getting you out of the way. The bo's'n, Pedro, says that your cousin suggested that Nunez should sail you out to sea, and then knock you on the head and heave you overboard. But Nunez would have none of that, and decided that he would carry you with him to Vera Cruz."

"And what will befall me at Vera Cruz?"

"He, being a pious man, will hand you over to the Holy Office."

"To the Holy Office! You mean the Inquisitors? And they —"

"They will burn you for a Lutheran dog, master."

We were both silent for awhile. I was thinking of naught but the fiendish cruelty which existed in such a man as Manuel Nunez. Presently I thought of Pharaoh Nanjulian.

"And yourself?" I said. "What will he do with you?"

"I am to share your fate, master. Senor Nunez is a good and pious son of Mother Church, and he will wipe out a score or two of sins by presenting the stake with two English heretics."

After that I thought again for a time.

"Pharaoh," I said at last, "we will not die very willingly. I have a good deal to live for. There is my sweetheart and my uncle to go back to, and also I have an account to settle with Jasper Stapleton. I will make an effort to do all this before my time comes."

"I am with you, master," said he.

"Have you thought of anything?" I asked.

"Nothing, but that we must escape," he answered.

"Could we manage that after the ship reaches Vera Cruz?"

"No, for a surety. We shall be watched as cats watch mice. If we ever set foot on a quay-side in that accursed port, master, we are dead men. God help us! I know what the mercies of these Spaniards are. I stood in the City of Mexico and saw two Englishmen burnt. That was ten years ago. But more of that anon. Let us see to the present. We are dead men, I say, if we set foot in Vera Cruz, or any port of that cruel region."

"Then there is but one thing for us," I said.

"And that, master?"

"We must leave this ship before she drops anchor."

"That is a good notion," said he, "a right good notion; but the thing is, how to do it?"

"Could we not take one of the boats some night, and get away in it?"

"Aye, but there are many things to consider. We should have to victual it, and then we might run short, for we should have no compass, and no notion, or very little, of our direction. We might starve to death, or die of thirst."

"I had as soon die of thirst or hunger, as of fire and torture."

"Marry, and so would I. Yea, it were better to die here on the wide ocean than in the market-place of Mexico or Vera Cruz."

"Let us try it, Pharaoh. Devise some plan. I will not fail to help if I can be of any use."

"I will think," he said; "I will think till I find a means of escape. I reckon that we have still a month before us. It shall go hard if our English brains cannot devise some method whereby we may outwit these Spanish devils."

So we began to plot and plan, spurred on by the knowledge of what awaited us in Mexico.

CHAPTER VII.

WE ESCAPE THE SPANIARDS.

Now that I knew his real sentiments towards me, it was very difficult to preserve my composure and indifference in the presence of Captain Manuel Nunez. As I sat at table with him, or talked with him on deck or in his cabin, I had hard work to keep from telling him my real thoughts of his wicked nature. Nay, sometimes I was sore put to it to keep my hands from his throat. Nothing would have pleased me better than to find either him or my cousin Jasper in some lonely spot where no odds could have favored them or me. Then my wrongs should have received full vengeance, and none would have blamed me for meting it out to these two villains. Judge how hard it was for me to have to associate, week after week, with one of the men who had so deeply wronged me, and, moreover, to have to preserve towards him a certain degree of cordiality. Try as I would, however, I could not give Nunez as much in the way of politeness as Nunez gave me. My manners were surly at the best, and I had much ado to preserve them at all.

Getting in the way of fair winds, we sighted the Bahamas, and passed the north-west coast of Cuba somewhere about the beginning of September. We were then some five hundred miles from Vera Cruz, but it was not until Christmas week that we bore down upon the Mexican coast. It was, I think, on Christmas morning that I first saw the shores of that beautiful land, whose natural loveliness served but to make more evident the horrible cruelties of the men who had seized and possessed it. Fair and wonderful it was as the mists lifted under the sun's warmth to see the giant peak of Orizaba lifting its head, snow-white and awful, into the clear air, while full seventeen thousand feet below it the land lay dim and indistinct, nothing more than a bank of gray cloud.

"You would think a country with such a mountain as that would be a place of much delight, master, would you not?" said Pharaoh Nanjulian, pointing to the great white peak. "It looks fair and innocent enough, but it is a very devil's land, this Mexico, since the Spaniards overran it; and yonder peak is an emblem of nothing in it, except it be the innocence of those who are murdered in God's name."

"What mountain is that?" I inquired.

"Orizaba, master. It lies some sixty miles beyond Vera Cruz, and is of a height scarcely credible to us Englishmen. God be thanked that there is so little wind today! With a fair breeze we should have been in port ere nightfall. As it is, we must take our chance tonight, master, or fall into the hands of the Inquisition."

"I am ready for aught," said I. "But have you thought of a plan?"

"Aye, trust me for that. Marry! I have thought of naught else since we came through the Bahamas. Certainly our chances are exceedingly small, for we must needs land in a country that is infested with our enemies, but we will do our best."

"Tell me your plan, Pharaoh."

"'Tis simplicity itself, master. Tonight it is my watch. When the captain is asleep in his cabin, do you come on deck and go aft. You will find a boat alongside, and into it you must contrive to get as you best can. Hide yourself there so that no one can see you from the deck. When the watch is changed, instead of going forward I shall make for the boat. No one will see me, I promise you. When I am with you we shall cut the boat adrift and let the vessel outsail us. Then we must make for the coast in the direction of Tuxtla. We shall know which way to steer because of the volcano. But after that — why, I know not what we shall do."

"Have you no plan?"

"Marry, I have ideas. We might go across country to Acapulco, hoping to find there an English ship; but 'tis a long and weary way, and what with Indians and wild beasts I fear we should never get there. Howbeit let us tackle one danger at a time."

Being then called to dinner I went below, and was perforce once more obliged to sit at meat with my jailer, who, now that his charge of me was coming to an end, was more polite than ever, and treated me with exceeding great courtesy.

"You have been on deck, Master Salkeld," said he, "and have doubtless perceived that we are in sight of land."

"I have seen the great mountain, Senor," I answered.

"True, the land is yet little more than a line. If the wind had been fair we should have dropped anchor ere midnight. Your voyage has been a long one, but I trust you have not been inconvenienced."

"Only as a man may be by the loss of his liberty, Senor."

"You will soon be free," he answered, giving me one of his strange, mocking smiles. "And I trust that when we part it will be with a full recognition on your side of the way in which I have carried out our bargain."

"As I do not remember our bargain, Senor, I am afraid that is hardly possible," I made answer.

"Chut! your memory is certainly at fault. However, the facts will probably occur to you — later."

"Part of the bargain, if I remember your first mention of it, Senor, was that you should carry me to the West Indies."

"You are right in that," said he.

"Are we approaching the West Indies?"

"The West Indies is a wide term, Master Salkeld. We are certainly not approaching the West India islands. We are, in fact, off the coast of Mexico, and the mountain you see in the distance is the famed peak of Orizaba. To-morrow morning we shall drop anchor in the port of Vera Cruz."

"And what shall I do there, Senor?"

He smiled at the question — a mysterious smile, which had a grim meaning behind it.

"Who knows, Senor? There are many occupations for a young and active gentleman."

Now, for the life of me I could not help asking him a very pertinent question before I left the cabin to return on deck.

"Senor," I said, "seeing that we are to part so soon you will perhaps not object to giving me some information. How much did my cousin, Master Jasper Stapleton, pay you for your share in this matter?"

He gave me a curious glance out of his eye corners.

"The amount of your passage-money, Master Salkeld, was two hundred English guineas. I hope you consider the poor accommodation which I have been able to give you in accordance with that sum."

"I have no fault to find with the accommodation, Senor," I replied. "So far as the bodily comfort of your prisoner was concerned you have proved yourself a good jailer."

"Let us hope you will never find a worse, Master Salkeld," he answered, with another mocking smile. "But, indeed, you wrong me in speaking of me as a jailer. Say rather a kind and considerate host."

I repressed the words which lay on the tip of my tongue ready to fling at him, and went on deck. The wind was still against us, and the ship made little progress, for which both Pharaoh and I were devoutly thankful, neither of us being minded to make Vera Cruz ere night fell. Certainly there was little to choose between the two courses open to us. If we were handed over to the Inquisitors by Nunez, we should certainly be burned at the stake, or, at any rate, racked, tortured, and turned over to a slave-master. If we reached shore we should have to undergo many privations and face all manner of perils, with every probability of ultimately falling into the hands of the Spaniards once more. Indeed, so certain did it seem that we should eventually meet our fate at the stake, or the rack, that more than once I doubted whether it was worth our while to attempt an escape.

But life is sweet, however dark its prospects may be, and a true man will always fight for it, though the odds against him are great. And, moreover, when a man knows what manner of death it is that awaits him, he will make the most desperate efforts to escape it, if it be such a death as that intended for us by the Spaniards. Now, although I had lived in such an out-of-the-way part of England, I had heard many a fearful story of the wrongs and cruelties practiced by the Inquisitors in Mexico. Tales came across the wide ocean of rackings and tormentings and burnings, of men given over to slavery, wearing their

San-benitos for many a weary year, and perhaps dying of torture in the end. We would do something to escape a fate like that, God helping us!

Late that night Captain Nunez stood by my side on deck. The wind now blew from the north-west, and the ship was making headway towards land. To the south-east, through the darkness, glimmered the volcanic fire of Tuxtla, but the giant peak of Orizaba had disappeared.

"Tomorrow at sunrise, Master Salkeld, we shall be in the port of Vera Cruz," said Nunez. "I have some friends there to whom I will give you an introduction. Till then, Senor, sleep well."

He smiled at me in the dim lantern light and went below. I remained pacing the deck for another hour. Once or twice I looked over the side and saw the boat swinging below our stern. Now, the poop of the Spanish ship was of a more than usual height, and I foresaw that I should have some difficulty in getting into the boat, and run a fair chance of drowning. Better drown, I thought, than burn; and so, after a time, the deck being quiet, I climbed over the side and managed to drop into the boat, where I made haste to hide myself as I best could.

It was some two hours after that when Pharaoh Nanjulian joined me, and immediately cut us adrift.

The ship seemed to glide away from us into the darkness.

CHAPTER VIII.

AN UNKNOWN LAND.

Now, although we were adrift in a perilous sea, and had no hope of making land, save in a wild and savage country, where there was more hope of mercy from the Indians than from the civilized Spaniards, I was yet so thankful to find myself free of the ship and of Senor Manuel Nunez, that for some moments I could scarcely believe in my freedom.

"I could swear that I am but dreaming and shall presently awake to find myself a prisoner," I said to Pharaoh, who was busily engaged in examining the boat.

"'Tis no dream, master," said he. "This is a very stern reality, as you shall quickly find. Nor is it time for dreaming. If we mean to come out of this adventure with whole skins, we shall have to acquit ourselves like true men."

"I am ready," said I. "Tell me what to do, and I will do it."

"Well said," he answered approvingly. "But I could see from the outset that you had the true spirit in you. You are a Yorkshireman, master, and I am a sea-dog of Cornwall; but, marry, we are both Englishmen, and we will come out of this scrape yet. 'Tis not the worst I have been in — but more of that anon. Now to begin with, we will discuss our present situation, and then, having determined our course of action, we will put it into execution."

So we talked things over, and eventually came to these conclusions. We were, so far as Pharaoh could reckon, about ten miles from land, and we must reach the coast during the night if we wished to escape observation. That accomplished, we must strike across country for

Acapulco, where it was possible we might meet with an English ship. The distance was some three hundred miles in a bee-line, and the character of the country rough; but that mattered little, for we should of necessity be obliged to keep away from the roads and bridges. There was no considerable town on our way, save Oaxaca, and that we must leave to our left. If we fell in with Spaniards we were lost men, for they would certainly carry us to Vera Cruz or to Mexico, and there hand us over to the Inquisitors. As for wild beasts and Indians, we must take our chance, trusting in God's mercy for protection and help.

We now examined the boat, which was but a small craft that had been unstrung the day before, in order that the ship's carpenter might examine some fancied defect in the rudder. Fortunately a pair of oars had been left in her, and these Pharaoh now took in hand, bidding me steer for the volcanic flame, which played over the peak of Tuxtla, immediately before us.

"I can pull ten miles in this sea," said he, "and I warrant you have had little experience in that line, master. Now, you see that the wind has drifted us due south until tonight, and therefore Nunez has come some five-and-thirty miles out of his course for Vera Cruz. He will now beat up along the coast, heading north and west, and so if we steer south-by-east he will have hard work to catch us when he finds that we are gone, as he will ere morning. And now to work."

Thereupon he fell to the oars, and with such good-will, that the light craft, her nose kept towards the volcanic fire, began to shoot through the regular swell of the placid ocean at a comfortable rate. Hour after hour he toiled, and would hear naught of my relieving him, though his throat grew dry with thirst and his arms ached. Gradually the coast loomed higher and higher through the gloom, and at length Pharaoh pulled in his oars, and stood up in the bow to look around him.

"When I was off this coast ten years ago," said he, "I remember a spot hereabouts where a boat might land with safety and ease. We will lie quiet till the light comes, master, and then attempt a landing."

"But suppose Nunez should see us?"

"He could not catch us ere we land if he did, unless by some strange chance he has gotten to the east of us — and that's not possible," said Pharaoh. "I reckon that by this time he is twenty miles to westward of us, and therefore we are well out of his reach."

So we hove-to until the morning began to break, when, spying a convenient creek, we ran the boat ashore, and so set foot on Mexican soil, wondering what was to befall us next.

Now, to me, who had never seen aught of any land save England, these new surroundings were exceeding strange and wonderful. Although it was yet but a half-light all round us on shore, the giant peak of Orizaba, rising high and magnificent across the land to the north-west, was already blazing in the saffron-colored tints of early morning, while directly above us the lower heights of Tuxtla also reflected the rays of the rising sun. Once away from the shore the vegetation surprised and delighted me exceedingly. Great trees, such as I had never seen or heard of, sprang from the rocks and towered above us like gigantic ferns; the undergrowth was thick and luxurious, and the grass under foot was soft and heavy as velvet. Also, though it was winter, there were flowers and plants blossoming in the open such as never blossom in our English glass-houses, so that altogether I was amazed at the richness and prodigality of the land, and said so to my companion.

"Aye," said he, "'tis indeed a fair land, master, and would be very well if these murderous Spaniards had left it alone. As it is, they have simply turned it into a pandemonium, such as all lands, fair or foul, become when men go a-lusting for gold and treasure. Yea, not even the Indians, with all their heathenish practices, were half so cruel as these Spaniards with their racks and thumbscrews, their stakes and daggers. And therefore the more reason why we should avoid them."

Having somewhat refreshed ourselves by a brief rest, and armed ourselves with two stout cudgels cut from a neighboring tree by Pharaoh's knife, which was the only weapon we had, we set forth through the woods, he leading the way. By that time we were faint with hunger and could well have done with a meal, but though there were, doubtless, Indian villages close at hand we dare enter none of them, and so went forward with empty stomachs. In the woods, however, we came upon prickly pears, which there grow wild, and these we essayed to eat; but had great difficulty in stripping them of the prickles, which, if they enter the tongue, do cause an unpleasantness that is not soon forgot. Our hunger growing very keen we sought to capture or slay some bird or animal, and Pharaoh being accustomed to this sort of hunting — for he had known many adventures — presently succeeded in knocking down a wild turkey, flocks of which bird we constantly encountered. We lighted a fire by means of his flint and steel, and cooked our quarry, and so went forward again refreshed by the food, which was pleasant enough to hungry men.

We pressed on for two days through the woods, living as we best could upon such animals as Pharaoh was able to knock down, and on the pears, which were all the more aggravating to our hunger because of their sharp spines. During those two days we did not come in contact with human beings, though we thrice saw parties of Indians and had to conceal ourselves from them. We followed no path, and if we chanced to cross one we immediately left it and plunged deeper into the woods. By the end of the first day our clothes were torn to rags, and hung in strips from our backs; by the end of the second our shoes had been cut to pieces, and so we looked as wretched and lost a couple of vagabonds as you ever saw.

On the evening of the second day we came to the verge of the wooded heights, and saw before us the wide plain of Orizaba, which lay between us and Acapulco, and must needs be crossed if we meant to reach the Pacific coast.

"It is here that I see most reason to be a-feared," said Pharaoh, as we halted and looked out across the plain. "There is precious little cover or shelter on this plain, and it will be a miracle if we escape observation in crossing it. Moreover, there are constantly traversing it bodies of Spaniards, going to and from Oaxaca and Mexico, so that we shall be liable to capture at any moment, having nowhere to hide ourselves."

"How would it do to hide ourselves as we best can by day, and to go forward by night?" said I.

"'Tis a good notion, master, and we will try it," he answered. "But I fear me there is little in which we can hide, and as for food, I do not see how we are to manage. Howbeit, we will not despair yet awhile, having managed so far."

That night we accordingly made our way across the wide and lonely plain, having for our guide the constellation Virgo, which Pharaoh Nanjulian knew and pointed out to me with some learning.

"Them that go down to the sea in ships," said he, "must needs learn a good deal if they would prosper. I have studied the heavens somewhat, because more than once it has been my lot to find myself at sea without a compass, and in a plight like that a knowledge of the stars and planets is a good thing for a man to have at his command. Now, if we do but set our faces to yonder constellation we shall keep in a straight line for Acapulco — and God send we may land there safely!"

We made fairly good progress across the plain, but when morning broke from the eastern horizon we were still many a long mile from the great terrace of mountainous land which divides Mexico from Oaxaca and the Pacific coast. Therefore we had to cast about us for some shelter. This we had great difficulty in securing, for the plain at that part was entirely barren of shrub or tree, and there was not even a water-course at which we could slack our parched throats. But coming upon a half-ruined hut, which had evidently been the home of some Mexican Indian, tending his sheep in those wild parts, we took refuge in it and lay down to sleep, hoping that no one passing that way would feel curious enough to stop and examine our shelter.

This sort of life continued to be our lot for another day and night, during which we had scarcely anything in the way of food, and also suffered severely from thirst. And what with this, and with our fear of meeting Indians and Spaniards materially increased, our condition was by no means a happy one. But we still continued to hope, and to cheer each other onward.

CHAPTER IX.

AN ADVENTURE OF SOME IMPORTANCE.

We traveled in this fashion, sleeping in the daytime and pressing forward during the night, until the sixth day after our departure from the ship. By that time we were both considerably changed in health and appearance. Our clothes were torn to rags, our feet and arms were torn and bleeding, and our vagabond air increased with every mile we covered. Of our looks, however, we thought nothing; but we were perforce obliged to think a good deal of our unfortunate stomachs, which had not been either filled or reasonably satisfied since we set foot in those regions. Hunger and privation, in short, were doing their work upon us, and we were doubtful if we should manage to hold out until we had crossed the country and made Acapulco.

Towards evening of the sixth day of our travels, we were lying asleep in a little gully formed by the descent of a mountain stream into the plain which we were then quitting. We had arrived at this spot early that morning, and finding sweet and fresh water there had drunk heartily of it and lain down to sleep in a sheltered spot. We were both well-nigh exhausted that morning, and our hunger was exceeding fierce; but sharp-set as we were our limbs refused to carry us on any foraging expedition, and therefore we sank to sleep, and slept despite our hunger and danger. It was well towards evening when I suddenly awoke. I know not what it was that made me open my eyes so suddenly, but there flashed through my mind at that moment a notion that we were being watched. It was a strange feeling, and one that occasioned me considerable discomposure, not to say fright, and it seemed to enter my brain with the same ray of sunlight that lifted my eyelids. And so strong was this feeling, that I experienced no surprise or astonishment when I saw two eyes looking straight into mine from over the top of a rock which rose immediately in front.

Nevertheless it was a hideous and fearful sight that I looked upon. The eyes shone, not out of a human face foul or fair, but out of the slits in a black cowl, drawn so tightly over its wearer's head that nothing of him was to be seen from forehead to chin. There was this horrible black thing, a blot upon the bright sunlit sky behind, peeping at me from over the rock, and out of its eye-holes gleamed two eyes, as keen and bright as those of a wild animal. If I had not just then been parched with thirst I should have screamed in my terror. As it was, I gave a feeble cry, and the black head instantly vanished. I leapt to my feet and ran forward to the rock. Below it the ground was broken and rocky, and at a few yards' distance was a belt of wood which stretched down to the plain. I fancied I could see a black robe disappearing amongst the trees, but though I waited a few moments I saw no further signs of a human being.

I returned to Pharaoh Nanjulian and woke him up. He was sound asleep when I touched him, but started to his feet as soon as I laid my hand on his shoulder.

"What is it, master?" he asked, scanning my face narrowly, as if he saw some sign of disturbance there. "You look alarmed."

"I have seen a man watching us."

"What kind of a man? Where has he gone?"

"Nay, that I know not. When I opened my eyes just now they fell full upon him. He stood behind that rock, peering over it at me. I saw naught of him but his head, and that was hidden in a black cowl with eye-slits, through which his eyes gleamed like fire."

Pharaoh shook his head.

"'Tis a Familiar," said he. "One of those accursed fanatics, master, that dog and pry after honest men like sleuth-hounds, and leave them not until the flame licks their bodies. This is bad news, i' faith. Which way went he?"

I told him that I thought I had seen a black robe vanishing among the trees below, but could not be certain. At that he seized his staff and went down the slope himself, examining all the likely places in which a man might have concealed himself. But he found naught, and so came back to me, shaking his head.

"You are sure you were not dreaming?" he asked. "Men dream of strange things when hunger is on them."

"How could I dream of what I never saw in my life?" said I.

"You mean the black hood, master? Alas! I have seen it, and so has many a good man, to his sorrow. Those accursed fanatics! They creep about in God's blessed sunlight like reptiles. You should see them walk the streets. Close to the walls they go, their hands meekly folded, their cowled heads bent to the ground, and yet their eyes note everything. God is on their lips — yea, but the devil is in their hearts."

"What shall we do, Pharaoh?" I asked him.

"Marry, all we can do is to leave this spot and push forward up the mountains. There are yet two hours of daylight, but we must chance that. If we can escape this fellow until darkness sets in, we may yet give him the slip altogether."

So we set out once more, our bodies refreshed by our long sleep, but the hunger still fiercely gnawing within us. We were driven to plucking the prickly pears again, troublesome as was the peeling of them, for we could eat them as we walked, whereas if we had gone a-hunting for wild turkeys or rabbits we should have had to light a fire, and that would have attracted attention to our whereabouts. However, we were successful in knocking down one or two birds, and these we took along with us, intending to cook them as soon as we considered ourselves in safety.

As night fell we emerged from the wooded slope up which we had painfully traveled, and found ourselves on a good road, evidently much used for traffic.

"This must be the highway that leads from Oaxaca to Vera Cruz," said Pharaoh, looking out upon it from a sheltering tree; "and lo! yonder is a post-house. We must bide awhile where we are or we shall be seen."

So we sat down amongst the undergrowth, which was there thick and luxurious, as it was in every wood we had yet crossed, and served to conceal us very well from observation. More than once, as we stayed there, we heard the voices of people passing along the highroad above, and we judged from that, that if we ventured to show ourselves upon it before nightfall we should certainly be seen and stopped. Therefore, apart from our usual hunger and discomfort, we were very well content to remain hidden until such time as the coast cleared.

Now about dark, and just as we were making up our minds to a fresh start, and wondering how we should fare in the mountainous range which we had yet to cross, there arose not far away along the highroad a chorus of shouts and screams of such exceeding bitterness, that we felt sure murder was being done. We leapt to our feet and advanced to the edge of the highway, but feared to go further lest we should be seen.

"'Tis some footpad affray," said Pharaoh, "and none of our business."

But just then came still shriller cries of entreaty for help, and they were so pleading and full of agony, that we both leapt into the road with one accord.

"That is a woman's voice," said Pharaoh. "We must needs go to her assistance, come what will. Have your staff in readiness, master, and if there is need, strike hard."

We ran swiftly down the road for some fifty yards, and then, turning a sharp corner, came suddenly upon the cause of the disturbance. In the middle of the highway stood a coach, drawn by two mules, and on either side of it were two tall fellows of ferocious aspect, striving to drag from it the occupants, who screamed for help without ceasing. There was no driver or servant visible; the rogues had doubtless escaped to the woods at the first sign of danger.

"Take the two on the left," said Pharaoh, "and get in the first blow, master. Look out for their daggers."

Now I had never been engaged in a fight since the days when Jasper and I occasionally came to fisticuffs with the village boys at Beechcot, but I felt my blood warm at the notion of combat, and so I sprang in between the two desperadoes who were busy at the left side of the coach, and laid my staff about their ears with hearty good-will. They were trying to drag an old man from the coach when we came up, and were threatening him with what I took to be the most horrible of curses. I hit one of them fair and square on the shoulder before he knew of my presence, and he immediately turned and fled, howling like a beaten dog. The other turned on me with a cruel-looking knife, but I knocked it out of his hand with a blow that must have broken his wrist, and he too fled into the woods with a fearful imprecation. Meanwhile, Pharaoh had beaten off his men on the other side; one was limping along the highway howling with pain, and the other lay on the ground senseless. We had carried the fight with sharp and startling effect.

Inside the coach sat an old gentleman and a young girl, and both were so frightened, that when we assisted them to alight they were nearly speechless, and could only sigh and moan. Presently, however, the young lady found her tongue, and began to pour out an astonishingly rapid flow of words to me, none of which I understood, but which I took to be expressions of gratitude.

"Say naught," whispered Pharaoh in my ear, "I will talk to them in their own lingo. Do not let them see that we are English."

"Noble gentlemen," said the old man, presently recovering his speech, "I know not how to thank you for this valuable assistance. Caramba! if you had not appeared when you did we should certainly have had our throats cut. Isabella mia, art thou safe? Did those knaves lay finger on thee?"

"They did but seize me by the wrist, father," answered the young lady. "But yourself — you are not hurt?"

"Nay, child, I called too loudly for that. But certainly another moment would have been our last. Senor, is yonder villain dead?"

"Nay," said Pharaoh in his best Spanish, "he breathes, Senor, and will come to presently."

"I am beholden, deeply beholden to you both, gentlemen. Dios! to think that I should be unable to travel on even so short a journey with safety! And my own servants — where are they, rascals and poltroons that they are. Ho! Pedro, Chispa, Antonio! I warrant me the knaves are hiding in these woods."

This was exactly the truth, for at the old gentleman's call three serving-men came forward from the trees and advanced tremblingly towards the coach. At sight of them their master flew into a terrible rage, and scolded them with a vigor which at any other time would have amused me highly.

"Cowards and knaves that ye are!" quoth he. "A pretty body-guard, indeed. What, ye pitiful rogues, did I not fit ye all out with pikes and pistols before quitting Mexico in case we met with ventures of this sort? Oh, ye poltroons, to fly me at the first glimpse of danger! And thou, Pedro Gomez, my coachman these ten years, fie upon thee!"

"Most noble Senor," said the man, trembling and bowing, "I did but run to find assistance."

"Thou liest, knave. Thou didst run to save thine own skin. But I will remember ye when we are safe in Oaxaca. I will have a convoy of soldiers over these mountains, and trust not to pitiful cowards like ye three. Tie me up this robber who lies there in the road, and fasten him behind the coach. We will see justice done on him at Oaxaca."

While the men were doing this the old gentleman once more talked to Pharaoh, thanking us again, and asking how he could reward us. Were we journeying to Oaxaca? If so, let us go along with him, and he would reward us bounteously for our protection.

"We thank your honor," said Pharaoh, "but we are two poor shipwrecked mariners, bound across country to Acapulco, where we hope to find ship. But if you would give us food and drink we would thank you, for in good sooth we are desperately hungered."

Now it luckily chanced that the coach was well supplied with both the commodities which we desired so earnestly, and, therefore, the old gentleman made haste to reward us according to Pharaoh's request, so that presently we found ourselves with our arms full of meat and bread and bottles of wine, our new-found friend pressing all upon us with great hospitality. Also, he would have us to take a purse of money, assuring us that we should find it useful, and as we had not a penny-piece between us we accepted this offering with thankfulness.

"I am sorry that ye cannot accompany me to Oaxaca," said he. "I should have been glad of the company of two such stalwart champions. But know, caballeros, that I am devoutly thankful to you, and will aid you if ever ye have need of me, and it lies in my power."

So we thanked him and said farewell for that time, and when the coach had gone on, taking the wounded prisoner with it, we continued our way up the mountains, first supping heartily of the food and wine, and blessing God for it.

"'Tis always well to help them that need help," said Pharaoh. "Verily we are rewarded for so doing. This meat and drink makes a new man of me, master."

And so it did of me, and it was well, for previously we had been sorely put to it to keep any heart or soul within our starving bodies.

CHAPTER X.

THE BLACK SHADOWS.

Our course that night being of more than usual roughness and difficulty, we made little headway, and by morning we had done no more than reach the height of the mountain range over which we were climbing, and which at that point was some three or four thousand feet above sea-level. Howbeit, we were not disappointed with our night's work, for when the sun rose we found ourselves looking out upon the wide plain which stretches from those mountains to the sea-coast of the Pacific. Half our journey was over.

"God send that all may be as well with us during this next journey as it has been during the last," said Pharaoh. "We have prospered exceeding well so far — yea, much better than I expected. Only let us do as well on our way over yonder plain and we shall reach Acapulco in safety."

"But what then?" I asked, not knowing what his plans might be.

"That," he answered, "is a difficult question, master. We shall certainly meet with no more love at Acapulco than at Vera Cruz, for the Spaniards have still some sore memories of the drubbings we have given them. But there we may find an English ship, for 'tis a convenient port for those vessels that come north. Maybe we shall have to wait awhile, and lie hidden outside the city or on the coast. All that we must leave till the time comes. 'Tis something that we have come thus far without let or hindrance."

And truly he was right there and we felt thankful to God for it. In truth we had so far been most mercifully protected, and our adventures had abundantly proved to us that God is merciful to men who have no hope of any mercy or consideration from their fellow-creatures.

We now sought out a convenient resting-place, and having found a quiet corner amongst the rocks, we sat down there and ate another hearty meal from the stores given to us by the old Spaniard, after which, feeling much refreshed, we lay down to sleep in a hopeful state of mind. The good food and drink had marvelously restored us, giving us new strength in body and soul, so that we now hoped where we had previously been inclined to despair. And so, being impelled to brighter thoughts than had filled our hearts for some days, we slept more composedly, and had none of those evil visions which had disturbed our sleep on former occasions.

Nevertheless evil was drawing near to us while we slept.

It was about half-way through the afternoon, when I woke with a sudden feeling that all was not well. It was not the feeling which I had experienced the previous day, namely, that I was being watched, but a curious sensation of coming ill. How it came into my mind I know not; all I know is that I suddenly awoke and came into possession of all my senses with startling swiftness, so that while I had been sound asleep one moment I was wide awake the next, and looking and listening with very eager and acute perception. Also, my heart was beating hard in my breast, as a man's heart will when he suddenly fronts some great danger. And then I knew that evil was at hand, and as I held up my head and looked round I saw it draw near.

The place in which we lay was a corner amongst the rocks on the side of the mountain. Before us lay a wide expanse of smooth stone, the top of a great rock that had its base in the woods below. Behind us rose a high wall of rock, and beyond that was the sun, now sinking towards the western horizon. Where we lay everything was in deep shadow, but the table-like piece of rock in front was bathed in brilliant sunlight, and when I woke and looked round my eyes fell upon it, and on a sight which was like to freeze my heart within me.

Some ridge of rock or mountain high above us was outlined on the bright stretch of reflected sunlight at our feet, and on this as I looked appeared two shadows — the shadows of human beings, standing motionless on the ridge, and evidently looking out from that commanding position across the wide plain that lay far below.

I recognized one of the shadows instantly. It was the figure of a man cloaked in some long clinging garment, that enveloped him from head to foot. As he turned his head I saw the peculiar cowl, with its peaked top, which had confronted me the previous day.

The other shadow seemed to be that of a naked man, of slender, sinewy limbs, who carried a bow, and whose head was ornamented with long, waving feathers. Now he stood motionless against the sky, looking like a figure cut out of stone or bronze; now he shaded his eyes with his hand, evidently gazing across the plain below; now he stooped and seemed to examine the ground at his feet. But the shadow of the cowled and cloaked figure stood statue-like and never moved.

Now, if you can so exercise your imagination as to put yourself in my place, you will not be slow to recognize the terror which came over me at this unexpected sight. If I had seen a dozen armed men spring out upon us from the rocks I should have cared not. But to see these sinister-looking shadows, motionless or restless, on the bright patch of sunlight, was an awful thing — yea, to this day I do often see it in my dreams, and wake sweating with fear and horror.

I leaned over and touched Pharaoh lightly. He woke on the instant and sat up.

"Hush!" I whispered, pointing to the shadows. "Look there!"

He lifted his hand to his brow and gazed at the shadows with a wonder-struck air. Then he seemed to recognize their import, and turned to me with a shake of the head.

"Lad," said he, "we are about to have trouble. 'Tis that accursed Familiar. He hath tracked us. Said I not that these devils in man's shape are like sleuth-hounds?"

"But the other, Pharaoh? What is the other?"

"An Indian, lad. See there, he is stooping to examine the ground. They are like dogs — they will find a trace where we should see naught."

"What shall we do?"

"God help us! — I know not. Once on our track they will hunt us down. See there!"

To the two shadows was suddenly added a third, a fourth, a fifth, then a sixth and seventh, and presently others until we counted twelve.

"All Indians except the monk," said Pharaoh. "He is the huntsman and they are his dogs. See, they are separating again. Lad, get thy cudgel in readiness. 'Tis the best weapon we have."

We started to our feet and gripped our staves firmly. And at the prospect of a fight my terror died away. There was no ghostly fear about things of flesh and blood. You can strike a man, but who can strike a shadow?

At that moment, over a rock to our left, appeared the face of an Indian, scarred and painted, a very devil's face to look at. We were seen at last!

CHAPTER XI.

CAPTIVE.

As soon as the Indian's face appeared above the rock Pharaoh and I instinctively moved towards him, whereupon he disappeared again with a sudden sharp cry, which was immediately answered from above.

"Now, we shall have the whole pack upon us," said my companion.

In this prediction he was right, for within a moment the whole body of twelve Indians had surrounded us, and stood gazing at us with faces in which I looked in vain for any sign of compassion at our forlorn state. Behind them came the monk, still clad in his shroud-like cowl, and moving with silent steps as if he were a ghost rather than a living man. But as he drew near to where we stood he threw back the hood from his head, and then we saw his face for the first time.

I will describe this man to you, because he was not only the most remarkable but also the most relentlessly cruel man that I have ever come across in my life. As for his name, which we learnt ere long, it was Bartolomeo de los Rios, and his one aim and passion was the hunting, torturing, and burning of heretics. He had the faculties of a sleuth-hound and the instincts of a serpent, and when he had once set his heart on hunting a man to his death, it was only by God's mercy that that man escaped.

Nevertheless this man as he stood before us, looking steadily upon us from under his cowl, did not seem so fearful a monster of cruelty as we afterwards knew him to be. We saw simply a thin, dark-faced monk, whose face was pale as parchment, and whose eyes were extraordinarily bright and keen. The lines and furrows on his brow and cheeks seemed to tell of pain or thought, and his tightly-pursed, thin lips betokened firmness and resolution. I think he could have stood calmly by while his own father was being tortured and have changed no muscle of his face. Thus he was an object of much greater fear than the Indians, who were certainly horrible enough to frighten anybody that had never seen them before.

We stood gazing at the monk and his Indians for a moment ere either of us spoke. The Indians seemed to wait instructions from the monk, and looked toward him with eager eyes. As for Pharaoh and myself, we waited to see what would happen. I think we both realized that fortune had suddenly deserted us, but nevertheless we kept a firm grip on our cudgels, and were both resolved to use them if necessary.

The monk spoke. His voice was low, sweet and gentle — there was naught of cruelty in it.

"Greeting, my children," said he, addressing us. "Be not afraid. There shall no harm come to you."

"It will be ill for the man who threatens us with any," answered Pharaoh in Spanish. "We are travelers, and have no mind to be disturbed."

"You travel by strange paths," said the monk. "To what part of the country are you going?"

"To Acapulco," answered Pharaoh, adding to me, in English, "there is no harm in telling him that."

"There is a good road from Oaxaca to Acapulco," said the monk. "Why not follow it?"

"We are minded to take our own way," said Pharaoh doggedly.

"You Englishmen are fond of that," observed the monk with a strange smile.

"Who says we are English?" asked Pharaoh.

"Your Spanish is proof of that."

"I am from Catalonia," said Pharaoh. "We do not speak pure Castilian there."

"And your companion? Is he, too, from Catalonia, or is he dumb?"

To that Pharaoh answered nothing. The monk turned his bright eyes on me.

"What is your business here?" he said, in very good English. "If you cannot speak to me in my tongue, I must talk with you in yours."

"Answer him," said Pharaoh. "There is no use in further concealment."

"I see no reason why I should answer you, master," said I, feeling somewhat nettled at the man's peremptory tone. "What right have you to stop us in this fashion?"

He smiled again, if that could be called a smile which was simply a sudden flash of the eyes and a tightening of the thin lips, and looked round at his Indians.

"The right of force," said he quietly. "You are two — we are many."

"Two Englishmen are worth twenty Spanish devils," said I sulkily.

"If it is to come to fighting," said Pharaoh, gripping his cudgel.

The monk said a word in a low tone. The Indians on the instant raised their bows and drew their arrows to the full extent of the string. The tips pointed dead upon us.

"Englishmen," said the monk, "look at those arrows. Every one of them is tipped with poison. If you move I give the word, and those arrows will find a resting place in you. Let them but touch your arms, your shoulders, inflicting but a scratch, in a few seconds you will be as one that is paralyzed, in a few minutes you will lie dead."

The man's words were gentle enough, but somehow his low, sweet voice made my blood run cold. Why did cruelty veil itself in such a honeyed tone?

"What is it you want of us, master?" asked Pharaoh presently.

"Your names and business."

"That is easily answered. This gentleman is one Master Humphrey Salkeld, of Yorkshire in England, who hath many powerful friends at court; as for me, I am a sailor, and my name is Pharaoh Nanjulian, of Marazion in Cornwall. As for our business, we are shipwrecked mariners, or as good, and our hope is to find an English vessel at Acapulco and so return home. If you be a Christian you will help us."

"Christians help only Christians. I fear ye are Lutherans, enemies of God."

"That we are not," answered Pharaoh stoutly. "I will say my Paternoster in English with anybody, and my Belief too, for that matter."

The monk sighed. Perhaps he was disappointed to find that Pharaoh had so much knowledge.

"And you?" he said, turning to me.

"I am a Christian," I answered, surlily enough, for I did not like this examination.

"We are both Christians, master," said Pharaoh. "Maybe we think not as you do on some points, but 'tis naught. So help us of your charity, and assist us to get out of this country to our own, and we will say a Paternoster for you night and morning."

"Verily," answered the monk, "you speak fairly. I will help you. You shall go with me to Mexico, and there we will see what ships there are at Vera Cruz."

"We would rather push forward to Acapulco," answered Pharaoh. "There are more likely to be English ships there."

"English ships have gone there little during recent years, and you will find none now," said the monk.

"For all that we would rather take our chance there," said Pharaoh.

"It will be better for you to accompany me to Mexico. Vera Cruz is close at hand. And now, as the day waxes late, we will proceed."

Now, there was no use in further argument, for the monk had every advantage of us, and was clearly minded to have us accompany him at whatever cost. Therefore we had to yield ourselves to his will but never did men give in with worse grace or heavier hearts than we.

"God help us!" said Pharaoh. "We are going into the very jaws of death in going to Mexico. We shall meet Nunez there, and even if we do not, we shall be handed over to the Inquisitors. But God's will be done. Moreover, while there is life there is hope. We may pull through yet."

So we set out, the monk going first and taking no further notice of us for some time. He would walk for hours as if absorbed in his own thoughts, and again for a long stretch of time he would read his book or count his beads, but to us he said little. He walked in the midst of the Indians, who for their part were kind and considerate to us, and indulged in no cruelties. Indeed, during our journey to the City of Mexico we had no reason to complain of discomfort or poor fare, for we had all that men can require, and were well treated, save that at night they guarded us more closely than we liked. But as to food and drink, we were abundantly served, and so began to wax fat, in spite of our anxiety.

There was no restriction placed upon our tongues at this time, and therefore Pharaoh and I talked freely whenever we were out of hearing of the monk. As for our conversation, it was all of one thing — the prospect that awaited us in Mexico.

"What will come of this venture, Pharaoh?" I asked him one day as we drew near our destination. "Shall we come off with whole skins, or what?"

"It will be well if we come off with our lives, master. I have been thinking things over today, and I make no doubt that this monk will hand us over to the Inquisition. Put no trust in what he says about finding us a ship at Vera Cruz. The only ship he will find us will be a dungeon in some of their prisons. Well, now, what are our chances when we fall into the hands of these fellows?"

"Nay, very small I should say. I am well-nigh resigned to anything. Nevertheless, Pharaoh, I shall make a fight for it."

"It may not come to fighting. Can you say the Paternoster, the Ave Maria, and the Creed?"

"I can say two of them, and I can learn the third. But what difference does that make?"

"All the difference 'twixt burning at the stake and wearing a San-benito in a monastery for a year or two. Now, if we are burnt there is an end of us, but if they put us into a monastery with a San-benito on our backs we shall still have a chance of life, and shall be poor Englishmen if we do not take it."

Thus we talked, striving to comfort ourselves, until at the end of the fourth day we were brought by our captors to the City of Mexico.

CHAPTER XII.

MORE CRUEL THAN WILD BEASTS.

There are times when, looking round these fair lands of Beechcot, and thinking on the quiet and prosperous life which I have spent in their midst these many years, I fall to wondering whether those dark days in Mexico were real or only a dream. It seems to me, sometimes, that all which then happened to me and to my companion, Pharaoh Nanjulian, must have been but a dream and naught else, so horrible were the cruelties and indignities practiced upon us. You could hardly bring yourselves to believe, you who have lived quiet, stay-at-home lives, how merciless were the men into whose hands we fell, and if I did but tell you one-tenth of the malignity which they displayed towards us, you would not wonder that I sometimes feel inclined to wonder if my memories of that most unhappy time are not dreams rather than realities. But I know well that there is nothing unreal about them, for I bear on my body certain marks which came there from the rack and the pincers, and there are moments when I seem to endure my agony over again, and the sweat drops from my brow as I think of it.

We were led into the City of Mexico through the gate of St. Catherine, and were thence marched forward to the Placa del Marquese, close by the market-place. There we were soon surrounded by a throng of folks, who seemed not unkindly disposed towards us. Some, indeed, brought us food from their houses, and others drink; one man handed Pharaoh Nanjulian a coat, a noble-looking lady, closely wrapped in her mantilla, gave me money, hurrying away ere I could refuse the gift. I suppose we looked so woe-begone and vagabondish in our rags and tatters, that the hearts of these people melted towards us. Nevertheless it was plain to see that we were prisoners, and that the monk had no notion of putting us in the way of getting a ship.

Now, as we stood there in the Placa, closely guarded by the Indians, the monk having disappeared for the moment, who should come up to us but that polite gentleman, Captain Manuel Nunez, arrayed in very brave fashion and smiling his cruel smile as usual. He pushed his way through the throng, folded his arms, and stood smiling upon us.

"So, Master Salkeld," he said, "you have fallen into the tiger's den after all. Certainly what was born to be burned will never be drowned. I looked to see you again, Senor."

"We shall possibly meet yet once again," said I. "And it may be where you and I are on level terms, Captain Nunez. If that time should ever come, ask God to have mercy upon you, for rest assured that I shall have none."

"Brave words, Senor, brave words! I wish it were possible that you might have the chance to make them good. But that I am afraid you never will have. You are safely caged."

Then he began to abuse us to the people, bidding them look upon us for English dogs, Lutherans, enemies of God, sweepings of the English sink of iniquity, for whom neither rack, thumb-screw, nor stake was sufficient reward. Me he denounced to the people as a runaway criminal, describing me in such terms as made my blood boil within me, and my hands itch to take him by the neck and crush the life out of his wicked heart.

"You are a liar and a knave," said I and then for the moment forgetting my dignity as an English gentleman I spat full in his face. Bethink you — my hands were tied behind me, and not free to use. Otherwise I had not done it.

Now at this insult his face turned deathly white and then flushed a bright red, and there came into his eyes a gleam which meant murder, and plucking forth his rapier he would certainly have slain me there and then, had not the monk returned at that instant and prevented his fury from wreaking itself upon me. At this interference he grew still more furious, and well-nigh foamed at the mouth, swearing by all the saints in his calendar that he would slay me where I stood. But at a word from the monk he smiled a grim, meaning smile, and thrusting back his rapier into its sheath turned away from us with a face full of hate and malignity.

We were now taken away to a hospital, where we found other Englishmen — some sailors that had been captured by the Spaniards at sea, and others merchants who had been taken while prosecuting their trade in various ports in that part of the world. Some of these men had been in captivity for many months, and they explained to us that they were being kept for a new sitting of the Inquisition, at which, they said, we should all be examined and possibly tortured, with a view to extracting from us confessions that would doom us to the fire. So under this prospect we sat down to wait, and for several weeks remained in strict captivity, having enough to eat, but being terribly cast down by the knowledge of what awaited us.

It appeared from such information as we could obtain that the Inquisitors were at that time absent from the city, conducting examinations in another part of the country, and that when they returned our cases would be gone into. There had been no Auto-de-fe, or public burning of heretics for a year or two, and it seemed only too probable from what we now heard that one was meditated for the coming Good Friday. Positive information on this point, however, we could not then get; therefore we remained in our captivity, alternately hopeful and despondent, praying God either to release us from our desperate situation or to give us strength to endure whatever might be in store for us.

About the beginning of Lent, in the year 1579, the Inquisitors returned to the City of Mexico, and it immediately began to be whispered amongst us that the examinations were shortly to begin. We soon found that this was the truth, and the first intimation of it came to us in highly unpleasant form. On Ash Wednesday we were removed from the hospital in which we had been confined until then, and were taken through the city to certain cells or dungeons, in which we were separately placed, so that from that time forward we saw nothing of each other, and thus had no companion to turn to for sympathy when our need was sorest. But as God would have it, it befell to Pharaoh Nanjulian and to me, that as we were being led across the market-square by our guards, there came up to us the old gentleman whom we had saved from highwaymen on the road to Oaxaca. He seemed vastly surprised to find us in that unhappy condition, and insisted with some slight show of authority on our guards allowing him to speak with us.

"Surely," said he, "ye are the two brave men who preserved me and my daughter from those cut-throat villains as we traveled to Oaxaca. How came ye in this company?"

"Sir," said Pharaoh, "that is what we do not know ourselves. We are two inoffensive Englishmen, brought into this country against our wills, and wishing or intending no harm to any man, but only anxious to find a ship that will carry us back to our own land. Here we are treated like malefactors and criminals, and yet we have broken no law that we know of, nor are we brought before any judge to hear what our jailer hath against us. If you indeed are grateful for what we did for you help us to our liberty."

"I am grateful, friend," answered the old man, "and will do what I can for you. But tell me your story."

So we told him all that had happened to us from the time of our leaving England, and mentioning more particularly the treacheries practiced upon us by Captain Nunez and Frey Bartolomeo, at the mention of whose names he shook his head.

"I am sorry indeed for you," said he when we made an end, "and the more so because ye are in a very grievous plight. But now, keep up your hearts, for I have some influence with the Chief Inquisitor, and it shall be exerted on your behalf. 'Tis truly a pity that ye are Englishmen, but I hope ye are Christians."

"Christians we are," said Pharaoh, "and will say our Paternoster and Credo with any man."

"'Tis well, and therefore keep up your hearts, I say. I will see to this matter at once."

This meeting and the cheerful words spoken to us by the old man did somewhat revive our hopes, more especially when we heard from our guards that he was a person of some distinction in that city. So we parted, Pharaoh and I, and were prisoned in solitary dungeons.

For the next three or four weeks I saw no man save my jailers, who fed me chiefly on bread and water, or on maize, crushed and boiled, which food did speedily bring me to a low and miserable condition. Indeed, what the noisomeness of my cell and the loneliness of my state failed to do the bad food speedily accomplished, so that within a month of my imprisonment I became a weak and nerveless creature, and was ready to weep at a rough word.

About three weeks before Easter I was taken before the Inquisitors and put to the question. Now, I had expected and dreaded this ordeal, and was not in over good a state to face it when at last it came upon me. Nevertheless I made shift to summon my courage so that I might show a bold front to my oppressors.

The Inquisitors sat in a small apartment hung round with black and lighted by torches, and there was that in their appearance which was calculated to strike terror into the stoutest heart. Behind a table, set upon a dais, sat the Chief Inquisitor, with his assistant on one side of him and his secretary on the other. They were all robed in black, and their thin, ascetic faces looking out from the dark recesses of their cowls, had in them neither mercy nor pity, nor indeed aught but merciless resolution. There were other robed and cowled figures in the room, but I noticed none of them particularly save the monk Bartolomeo, who stood there ready to make accusation against me.

There was an interpreter in the apartment, a half-breed named Robert Sweeting, whose name I desire to put on record, because he did me a kindness at the risk of his own life. To this man the Inquisitors addressed their questions, and through him I answered them to the best of my ability.

They set out by asking me the full particulars of my presence in Mexico, which questions I replied to with very great delight, as they afforded me an opportunity of having my say as to Captain Manuel Nunez and his fellow-villain Frey Bartolomeo, whom I did not spare, though he stood by and heard me with an unmoved countenance. Indeed, I spake so plainly concerning him that the Chief Inquisitor stopped me.

"It is not seemly," said he, "to speak in disrespectful terms of men vowed to sacred offices."

To this I answered that I had been brought up from my birth to treat my pastors and teachers with respect and reverence, but that I could feel none for a man who had abused his sacred office by deceiving unfortunate men.

Then they began to examine me as to my faith, and commanded me to say the Paternoster, Ave Maria, and the Creed in Latin, which, rubbing up such Latin as I remembered from Mr. Timotheus Herrick's instructions, I made difficult shift to do, informing them at the same time that I could say all these things much more readily in English. And this part of my examination being over, and my judges seeming satisfied, I began to breathe more freely, hoping that all might end well.

But now they began to examine me on more particular and nicer points, and it was plain to me that if I did but make a slip they would visit it upon my body. For they demanded first, whether I believed or not that any bread or wine remained in the paten or in the chalice after the consecration, and second, whether or not the bread and the wine were not actually the very body and blood of our Lord. To have answered "No" to these questions would have insured my death, therefore I cudgeled my brains for a fitting reply to them, well knowing what depended upon it. And bethinking me of the articles and teachings of my own church, I made answer that I was no scholar or theologian, but a simple country gentleman that had left subtle points to priests and schoolmen, and had always held what they taught me, namely, that our blessed Lord is indeed verily and truly present in the sacrament of His body and blood. This answer seemed to satisfy them, but presently they asked me if I did not follow the teachings of Doctor Martin Luther. I cheerfully replied to that, that I knew naught about Doctor Luther, and had never heard his name mentioned until I came into Mexico; which was plain truth, for we were out of the world at Beechcot, and knew naught of controversies. Then they would have me to tell them what I had been taught to believe in England, to which I answered that I had never been taught any other doctrine than that to which I had already testified, and in which I did firmly and truly believe as a good Christian man, hoping for salvation in the Christian faith.

"We must have a more satisfactory answer than that," said the Chief Inquisitor, "otherwise we must try what a sterner method will do with you."

"Sir," said I, "other answer I cannot give you, for I have already told you the truth. As for my sins against God I heartily ask His forgiveness, and also yours if I have offended your laws in any way; but I beseech you to remember that I came into your country against my own will, and have never done aught against its laws or against you wittingly. Therefore, I beseech you to have Christian mercy upon my defenseless condition."

But they had none, and that night I was put upon the rack, and cruelly tortured by Frey Bartolomeo and his fellows, in the hope that I should confess something against myself. However, God giving me strength, I said naught, and was preserved through that awful torment, the memory of which is strong in my mind even after all these years.

CHAPTER XIII.

THE AUTO-DA-FE.

About the beginning of Holy Week the Inquisitors caused to be erected a great scaffold against the large church in the main square, and from it they proclaimed, with much beating of drums and blaring of trumpets, that whoever should come there upon Good Friday should have made known to them the most just judgments of the Holy Inquisition upon the English heretics, Lutherans, and should, moreover, see the same put into immediate execution. And so now we were face to face with whatever final cruelty these devils in human shape might devise upon us, who were helpless and defenseless in their hands.

There was little rest for any of us on the night preceding the judgments, for there came to each of us officers and Familiars of the Inquisition, tormenting us with gibes and sneers, and bringing us the San-benitos in which we were to appear in the great square next morning. It was already turning gray in the east when two of these men entered my dungeon, where I lay still stiff and bruised because of the racking which I had undergone a few days before. They woke me rudely and without consideration, caring naught for the woes I had already suffered or the sorrow I was that day to undergo.

"Wake, English dog, Lutheran, enemy of God!" cried one. "Wake and robe thyself to meet thy master the devil. Truly the saints will rejoice to see the sight provided for them this day."

Then they hustled me from my straw pallet and bade me dress in the San-benito, which was a garment of yellow cotton having divers devices painted upon it. And this done they took me out into the courtyard of the prison, and there for the first time for some weeks I met Pharaoh Nanjulian. It was easy to see, even in the uncertain light of the early morning, that he had undergone the same torments which they had applied to me. His face was pinched and thin with suffering, and his great frame seemed to have been crushed and bruised until it had shrunk in height and girth. Yet he bore himself with composure and bravery, and I felt at once that, however the rest of us behaved, he at least would not disgrace the name of England.

"Heart up, master!" quoth he, as soon as we came within speaking distance of each other. "Heart up! Let us show ourselves brave men this day. I do not think they can torment us more than they have already done. And what if they kill us? We must all die."

"Did they torture you badly, Pharaoh?" I asked, admiring his fortitude.

He shook his head and smiled grimly.

"So badly, master, that it seemed as if every bone in my body was broken and every sinew cracked. But a man may undergo a deal of suffering and yet live. So let us quit us like men and be strong. For truly, though we be in the hands of these devils at present, God is near us, and will maybe be nearer ere the day is done."

Then our custodians separated us again, and for a couple of hours they exercised us in the prison yard, showing us in what order we should proceed to the scaffold, and admonishing us as to our behavior when we had come there. And after that was over, it being broad daylight, they gave us breakfast, which was a cup of wine with a piece of bread fried in honey, and so we were ready for the ordeal.

There were some sixty to seventy prisoners in all, of all nationalities, a considerable number being Englishmen, and all of us were dressed in those hideous San-benitos, which make the most shameful garb that a man can wear. Being drawn up in single file, our guards fastened a halter round the neck of each prisoner, and afterwards gave to each of us a green wax candle, which we carried, unlighted, in the right hand. Two Spaniards, well armed, guarded each of us, and so the procession being arranged, the great doors were thrown open and we were led forth into the square.

The crowd in the square was so thick that the guards had much ado to free a passage through it; but ere long we came to the scaffold, and were conducted upon it, seating ourselves on long rows of chairs placed in full sight of the people. We had not long occupied this shameful position when the Viceroy and his officers came upon the scaffold by another flight of steps, closely followed by the Inquisitors, who took the chief places and made much show of their authority. Then three hundred friars, wearing the garb of their various orders, black, white, gray, and brown, were marshaled to their places, and all was ready for the judgments.

Now, we were so sorely exercised in our minds at that time because of the agony of sitting there and wondering when our turn would come and what our fate would be, that I have utterly forgotten many of the names and sentences of my unfortunate companions. Some still come back to me, because their sentences were heavier than those which have escaped my memory.

The manner of judgment was after this fashion. The clerk to the Inquisitors calling out our names in a loud voice, we were commanded to stand up in our places and hear the judgment of the Holy Office upon us.

Thomas White, Cornelius Johnson, Peter Brown, Henry More, all Englishmen shipwrecked on those inhospitable coasts or captured at sea, were condemned to three hundred lashes on horseback, and to serve in the galleys for ten years.

William Collier, Thomas Ford, John Page, two hundred lashes and eight years in the galleys.

Stephen Brown and Nicholas Peterson, a Dutchman, one hundred lashes and six years in the galleys.

Then came some forty or fifty men whose names I have forgotten, who were condemned to a lesser number of lashes and less servitude in the galleys, and after them some four or five who were adjudged to serve in monasteries for various terms of years, wearing their San-benitos all the time.

And then, after two or three hours of weary waiting, for they did everything with exceeding tediousness and much ceremony, they called upon Pharaoh Nanjulian and myself, and we stood up together to receive sentence. And then we suddenly knew that God had not deserted us, for the sentence was a lighter one than any that we had heard passed. We were to serve two years in the galleys, submitting ourselves to the chaplain for admonition and instruction. So that was over and we could breathe freely again.

Nevertheless the horrible work of that day was far from over, for it was hardly begun. The torments, the murders, were yet to come.

William Moor, John Wood, and Hans Schewitzer, a German Lutheran, were brought up for sentence and condemned, being pestilent and naughty heretics, to be burned to ashes.

They lost no time, these villainous Spaniards, in carrying out this sentence. In front of the scaffold stood three stout iron posts, firmly sunk in the ground, with fagots already piled about them, and to these the unfortunate men were speedily bound, amidst the silence of the crowd and the cries of the monks and Familiars, who pressed upon their victims, bidding them repent and recant ere they were lost forever. But to these murdering villains the three men answered naught, and presently it was all over with them, and there was one more crime recorded against Spain.

Then those of us who had been sentenced to so many lashes were led down from the scaffold and placed upon horses, being stripped to the waist, and having by them, every man, an executioner armed with a whip. Such of us as had escaped this sentence were arranged in pairs behind, with our halters still round our necks and our guards on either side of us. Before the men who were to be whipped marched two criers, crying "Behold these English dogs, Lutherans, enemies of God," and at intervals came Familiars, such as Frey Bartolomeo, admonishing the executioners to lay on and spare not. Then the procession started, and was conducted by the criers through all the principal streets back to the great square, and at every few steps the executioners laid on with their whips, fetching blood at every stroke, so that to any man having aught of mercy and compassion within him the spectacle was horrible and nauseating, though to the Familiars and Inquisitors it seemed delightful enough.

Now, as we returned to the great square, this bloody work being over, the throng pressed upon us so closely that for some few moments we were unable to move, and while we stood there waiting for what would happen next, there came to our side Captain Manuel Nunez, his evil eyes mocking and sneering at us.

"So, Master Salkeld," said he, "it would seem that you have not altogether escaped. Our Holy Office is merciful, Master Salkeld, yea, sadly too merciful for my liking. But there are those of us, who know not any mercy for Englishmen and heretics, as you shall find ere long, both of you."

With that he vanished in the crowd, and presently Pharaoh and I were led back to prison, wondering what his last words meant.

CHAPTER XIV.

ON BOARD THE GALLEY.

Being led back to the prison, Pharaoh and I found to our unspeakable joy and astonishment that we were to be placed in one cell and not separated as heretofore. This consideration on the part of our jailers was exceedingly pleasant to us, because it afforded us the opportunity of conversing one with the other. Therefore, in spite of our bruises and strains, caused by the rack and not yet forgotten, and of the sad sights which we had that day seen, we made an effort to pluck up our spirits, and to be cheerful and even hopeful.

We were further assisted in this laudable desire by a visit from the old gentleman whom we had rescued from highwaymen on the road to Oaxaca. About seven o'clock that evening he was admitted to our cell, and left alone with us. This latter fact at once assured us that our friend was a man of rank and position, otherwise he would not have been permitted to see and speak with us, save in the presence of witnesses.

"I trust all is well with you, friends," said he, as he entered our presence, and set down a basket which the jailer had carried to the door. "I come to see you at a sad time, doubtless, but 'tis indeed with feelings of friendship."

"We have so few friends in this country, Senor," answered Pharaoh, "that we are glad to see any of them. Nay, indeed, so far as we know, your honor is the only friend we have. Therefore, Senor, you are something more than welcome."

Now the jailer being gone, the old gentleman took our hands in his own, and was like to weep over us, at which we marveled, for we did not know that his gratitude was so hearty, seeing that we had done such a small thing for him.

"Alas, friends," said he. "I grieve for you more than I can say, for I hate and abominate these murderous Inquisitors, whose hearts are filled with naught but torment and murder. Nevertheless I have saved you somewhat, for it was through my efforts and bribes that you came off with such light sentences."

"I thought we had your honor to thank for that," said Pharaoh. "Aye, 'tis well to have a friend at court when need arises."

"I labored hard," said the old gentleman, "to secure your freedom, but these bloody-minded Inquisitors are without bowels of mercy, and ye are fortunate to have escaped death or torture. But now I have brought you a little matter of wine and fruit, so fall-to and refresh yourselves, and after that we will talk of what is to come."

So he unpacked his basket and set food and wine and delightful fruit before us, and we ate and drank and were vastly comforted thereby, for our commons during the past week or two had been of the very shortest. And when we had thus refreshed ourselves, we began to discuss our situation anew.

"That you have escaped with your lives and without the torture of the lash," said our friend, "is due to my continued exertions on your behalf. But now, gentlemen, I am powerless to do more for you."

Then we once more thanked him for doing so much, saying that we should always hold his kindness in remembrance, and should ever pray for his happiness and prosperity.

"And if," continued I, "your honor can suggest any means by which we can escape from these galleys and regain our own country, we shall be further beholden to you. For, indeed, we have friends in England who must be anxious about us, if they be not already in despair of ever seeing us again."

"I fear there is small chance of your escape," said he, shaking his head. "Men that are chained to the oar cannot well escape. I pray God that you may survive your two years of that work — it is not all that do."

"Sir," said Pharaoh, "do you know where we shall be taken?"

"Nay," answered he, "that I cannot say. Most men who lie under your sentence are shipped to Spain, and are there placed in the galleys. The same fate is probably in store for you."

"God help us if they take us to Spain!" said Pharaoh. "We shall have to go through it all over again."

However, it seemed almost certain that this would be our fate, and as nothing that we could say or do could alter it, there was naught for it but to submit ourselves with such cheerfulness as we could muster. But here the old Senor gave us some additional comfort, for it seemed that his special purpose in coming to us that night was to give us the names of friends of his in certain towns and ports of Spain, to whom we might apply in case of our being in their neighborhood.

"You are something more than likely to be finally dismissed at Cadiz or at Seville," said he, "and it will be none the worse if you know where to turn for a friend;" and with that he gave us the names of certain Spanish gentlemen of rank, his friends, assuring us that they would help us to escape to England. And these names he made us learn by heart, and then, having no more time to spend with us, he bade us farewell, and we saw him no more. But in him we found one Spaniard at least who hated the horrible practices of the Inquisitors, and had a heart within him which was not insensible to the woes of others.

After we had remained in the prison five days longer, we were one morning brought forth and stripped of our San-benitos and given rough clothing suited to galley slaves. And that being done we were mounted on stout horses, in company with the other prisoners who had been sentenced to serve in the galleys, and being guarded by a great number of soldiers, well armed, we were sent off across country to the port of Acapulco. But ere we left Mexico every man of us had fastened to his left wrist and ankle a heavily-weighted chain, which would have made it impossible for us to attempt an escape even if we could have eluded the vigilance of our escort.

We were somewhat surprised to find that our first destination was Acapulco, for we had fancied that we should be sent to Vera Cruz, which is much nearer to the city of Mexico, and from which we expected to be sent across seas to Spain. We found, however, that at Acapulco there lay at that time a great treasure-galleon, the Santa Filomena, which the Spaniards were minded to take home by way of the Pacific islands and Africa, it being their belief that by this route there would be less chance of meeting Hawkins, or Drake, or Frobisher, or any of the great English sea-captains, of whom they were mortally afraid. In this galleon, then, we were to be shipped, with the prospect of a long and tedious voyage, which, according to Pharaoh's calculations, might cover the best part of a year even with fair winds.

Our overland journey to Acapulco was not wholly unpleasant, for our guards being soldiers, and free from the encouragement of those murderous fanatics the Inquisitors and Familiars, treated us with as much consideration as was possible, and forbore to taunt us with our misfortunes. Moreover, we were frequently lodged for the night in the neighborhood of some convent or monastery, and then we did exceeding well, the friars feeding us with their best, and compassionating us for our many sorrows. And at that time it was plain to us that the Inquisition was heartily hated by the friars — black, white, and gray, — and met with no favor from any but such as had long since forgotten all that they had ever known of mercy and compassion.

Having reached Acapulco, after many days' journeying over mountains and plains, we were immediately conveyed on board the Santa Filomena, which was a great galleon of full rig, having a high poop and a double bank of oars, and there our chains were knocked off by the armorer. This relief, however, did not long benefit us, for we were presently conducted below to a great deck filled with long wooden benches, parallel with the mighty oars which came through the ports. To one of these benches Pharaoh and I were immediately chained and padlocked, our companions suffering a like treatment. In another part of the deck the benches were filled by negroes, stark naked, whose backs and shoulders were covered by scars, and who yelled and grinned at us like fiends or madmen.

"God help us!" said Pharaoh; "they will not release us from these benches till we make Seville or Cadiz."

And at that awful prospect I half-regretted that we had not died in Mexico. For simply to think of being chained to the oar all those weary months amidst that foul and unclean mass of humanity, sleeping where we labored, and eating amidst dirt and filth, was more than I could stomach, and at that moment black despair seemed to settle upon my heart. But Pharaoh once more came to my aid and strove to cheer me.

"Heart up, master!" said he. "All is not yet over. We are going through sore trials, but what then? Are we not Englishmen? At any rate let us show a stern front to these villains. Cowards we will never be."

CHAPTER XV.

NUNEZ IN A NEW GUISE.

The second day after our arrival at Acapulco, we knew by the hurry and scurry on board our vessel that preparations were being made for sailing. Our deck was now full, and every oar was fully manned with its complement of slaves or captives. Of these the majority were blacks, whose misfortunes had transformed them into nothing better than wild animals; but there were still a large number of whites, and amongst them thirty to forty of our own countrymen. Every man was chained to his bench, and it was evident that there was no intention of releasing us until our voyage came to an end. Thus amongst our miserable company were many who hung their heads in deep dejection, and envied the three men who had met death by the flames in the great square of Mexico.

Towards the evening of that day, as I was sitting lost in sad thoughts, I looked up and saw standing at my side two figures, which I had given anything rather than set eyes upon. One was that of Captain Manuel Nunez, the other the black-robed form of Frey Bartolomeo. They stood regarding me steadfastly: the monk calm and quiet, the sailor with his usual cold smile faintly curling about the eyes and mouth.

"So, Master Salkeld," said Nunez, "we meet again. You are doubtless on your way home to England to take vengeance on your cousin, Master Stapleton."

I looked at him steadfastly. I was not going to be cowed by him, defenseless as I was.

"That may be, Senor," said I. "It is a long way to England by the road we are taking, but I shall reach it if God wills that it should be so."

"You do well to make that proviso," said he. "For God gives His power to men, and at this moment I, as master of this vessel, and Frey Bartolomeo, as its chaplain, are his viceregents. Wherefore, Master Salkeld, I think your chances are not good."

"We are in God's hands," said I; though indeed my heart turned faint and sick to think that these wretches had us in their power.

"At present, good Master Salkeld, you are in mine," he answered, smiling mockingly upon me. "But then you know what a kind and considerate host I am. You did admit that, when I carried you across the Atlantic. Still, Master Salkeld, things are somewhat altered between us. I am not now paid to carry you to Mexico and get rid of you. Also, since then you have spat in my face. Ah, you remember that, do you? Dog, you shall remember it every day of your life! I will not kill you now, as I might, but I will kill you by inches, and you shall die at last at your bench and lie there to rot. That is the fate of the dog who spits in the face of a Spanish gentleman."

So he turned away, but the man sitting next me put out his hand and plucked the monk's cloak, bidding him remember that he had promised to find him a ship for England, and begging him to keep his plighted word. But Frey Bartolomeo shook him off.

"Thou art a heretic," he said. "With heretics we keep no faith. To thy oar, Lutheran!"

CHAPTER XVI.

THE FLAG OF ENGLAND.

And now our cup of misery seemed full indeed. We were friendless and captive, and we had for our jailers two of the most inhuman beings that ever lived to disgrace the earth, and both of them hated us with an exceeding bitter hatred; one because I had spat in his face, the other because we had escaped the fire. Moreover, we were chained to an oar in a vessel which was sailing over I know not how many thousands of miles of water, in latitudes where it was not likely we should fall in with any ship that could rescue us. Verily there seemed before us nothing but horror and death!

And truly our lot was hard. Hour upon hour we tugged at the oar. Where we toiled there we slept, amongst the shrieks, sobs, groans, and heart-rending lamentations of our fellow-captives. Up and down the gangways that divided us walked stalwart Spaniards, armed with heavy whips, which they scarcely ever ceased from laying about our bare shoulders. Our food was such as is given to pigs in England — coarse maize or meal, soaked in cold water, with bread of the blackest and hardest description. The heat burned us to madness; the cold night-winds blew in upon us; the salt-spray dashing through the open ports found the raw places in our wounds and stung us as if with fire. Verily, we were in hell! Ere many days had gone by a man dropped and died at his post. They let him hang there by his chains till another day had gone past, then they knocked off his irons and flung him through the port-hole. And there was scarcely a man of us that did not envy him.

Now that Captain Manuel Nunez had us in his power there was apparently no limit to his cruelty. Scarcely a day passed on which he did not descend the ladder to our deck and vex our souls with some new form of torture. Sometimes he would take his station near us, and bid the overseers lay on to us with their whips. Sometimes he would take the whip himself and beat us about the head and face with it until we became senseless. Now and then he would amuse himself by pricking us with his sword or dagger; now and then he would spit in our faces and bespatter us with filth, pouring out upon us every foul and evil name he could think of. And when he had worked his will upon us, there would come to us Frey Bartolomeo, cold and cruel, and he would admonish and instruct us, and finding that he could get naught out of us, would depart cursing us for Lutherans and dogs.

These two presently devised a new torture, and put it into operation upon us. They caused the ship's armorer to make an iron brand, bearing the word "Heretic", and this being heated red, they came down to us and branded us on back and breast, so that all men, they said, should know us for what we were. And after that they gave us more lashes, and then deluged us with salt water, and so left us more dead than alive.

Now, after I had undergone some weeks of this treatment, I was like to have lost my senses, for the strength of my body was giving out, and I felt myself powerless to resist the continued cruelties and insults which were put upon me. Yea, I should certainly have gone mad at that time if it had not been for my faithful companion, Pharaoh Nanjulian, who did his best to cheer and support me, and got no reward for it but an increase of blows and stripes from Nunez, and venomous curses from Frey Bartolomeo.

It was one of Nunez's chief delights at this period to come down upon our deck and goad me into a rage that closely approached madness. Thus after exposing me to numerous insults, he would ask me what I proposed to do when I reached England again, and what fate I was keeping in store for my cousin Stapleton.

"It must afford you the most exquisite delight of which the human mind is capable, Master Salkeld," he said one day, when he had tormented and plagued me beyond endurance, "to sit here in these pleasant quarters and think of your cousin at home. He hath doubtless entered upon the family estates and married the lady whose affections you stole from him, and maybe he hath by this time told her of the trick he played upon you, and they laugh at it together."

And at that I cursed him before God and man and wept bitter tears, for I was thoroughly broken, and had no more heart in me than a child.

"So you are broken at last?" said he, and struck me across the mouth and went away.

And then I wished to die, for I was indeed broken; but Pharaoh did his best to console me and bade me be of good cheer, for we should triumph yet.

Now the next day, our voyage having then lasted some nine or ten weeks, we were aware of a sail bearing down upon us from the south-east, and before long it became evident that this ship was chasing us, whereupon there was much to-do on board the Santa Filomena, and our overseers urged us to renewed exertions with continual lashing of their whips. Nevertheless, within three hours the ship had overhauled us, and from our post we saw flying from her mast-head the flag of England.

CHAPTER XVII.

FRANCIS DRAKE.

Now, if you can bring yourself to imagine what he feels like who, having remained in dire and horrible distress for many weary days, suddenly sees salvation coming to him, you will know what we felt as we gazed through the port-hole and saw that noble English ship draw near with the English flag flying at her mast-head. If you have ever been in like peril yourself you will understand it better. A man condemned to die and suddenly reprieved; another suddenly released from awful slavery; a third suffering from heavy sorrow and suddenly overwhelmed with good tidings — any of these will know what we felt.

"An English ship!" cried Pharaoh. "Thanks be to God — an English ship!"

And straightway there rose from the crowded benches on our deck a strange and marvelous babble of sound. Some burst into tears of thankfulness and relief, some howled like wild beasts because of their chains, some cursed and blasphemed because there was small chance of the English ship's folk knowing our condition. Others shouted and yelled for help; the men sitting next the port-holes thrust forth their heads and cried loudly across the waters, though the ship was yet a good mile away. Every man betrayed his emotion and his misery in some way: here they tugged at the chains which bound them, there they showed their teeth at the Spaniards, snarling and snapping like dogs chained to a staple in the wall. And then the overseers fell upon us once more, and their great hide-whips descended mercilessly upon our shoulders, so that we were forced to tug at the oars with redoubled force, and the galleon shot forward again under a storm of yells and cries and loud groans.

"Yon is an English ship, as I live," said Pharaoh, as we tugged at our oar. "And she will overhaul us. Pray God she does not slay a score of us in this rat-trap by her first shot. If she only knew what we know. Listen, master!"

Over the strip of sea that separated us came the dull, heavy roar of a cannon-shot. They were firing at us in order to make the Spaniard lay-to. But Captain Manuel Nunez had no intention of acceding to the Englishman's wishes in that respect, and it was evident that he was crowding on all sail, and making every possible effort to escape that terrible ship which overhauled him hand over hand. On deck we heard the Spaniards rushing hither and thither, the mates and boatswain shrieking and yelling orders to the crew, the armorer and the soldiers making ready the ordnance and small arms. Now and then we caught the voice of Nunez, cool and collected as usual, but very fierce and determined; and once the pale face of Frey Bartolomeo appeared, and we heard him admonishing the overseers to lay on with their whips.

"We are like to be flayed alive if this goes on much longer," muttered Pharaoh as the lash curled about his shoulders again. "Oh, if we were but free and had some weapon in our hands! Lay on, ye murderous villains, lay on! Your reign is well-nigh over. Master, hold up a while longer. See there!"

Another puff of white smoke burst from the English ship's side, followed by a dull roar, and, immediately after, by a loud crashing and splintering of the deck above our heads. Then came shrieks, groans, and loud cries of pain. The shot had swept the deck. Fathom by fathom the English ship overhauled us. Through our port-hole we could see her deck swarming with men armed to the teeth. On her poop stood a little knot of men evidently in command, and one of these was directing the boatswain with outstretched arm.

"I see their plan," said Pharaoh; "they have seen the oars, and they are minded not to fire upon us again for fear of killing or wounding the captives. They are going to lay their ship alongside ours and board us."

So the ship came nearer and nearer, sailing nearly twice as fast as our great lumbering galleon, and at last we could make out the faces of the men on deck. And suddenly Pharaoh set up a great cry that made every Englishman on our deck turn to him with astonishment.

"'Tis Francis Drake!" he cried. "God be thanked, 'tis Francis Drake himself! See yonder, lads, there he stands on the poop. Are there any men here that ever served under Francis Drake? If so, let them look out at yonder captain and speak."

"'Tis Francis Drake and no other!" cried one. "I know him by the gold band round his scarlet cap. He always wears that at sea. Now may God be praised for this deliverance."

But there was much to be done ere our deliverance could be accomplished. Nay, indeed, it seemed as if our cruel jailers were minded to murder us before ever help would come, for they proceeded to beat us so unmercifully with their whips that many of us sank down faint and bleeding, and lay like dead men. But the rest of us kept up because of the fierce excitement.

Presently the English ship was within a boat's length of us, and then she slowly crashed against our side, the brass muzzles of her guns, in some cases, coming through our ports. Meanwhile the Spaniards had not been idle, for their gunners were plying their cannon with all possible speed, and the noise and confusion was horrible. But yet never a shot did the Englishman fire, but their ship closed steadily upon us. At last we heard the grappling-irons thrown out and made fast, and knew that the two ships were locked together, like lions that fasten teeth and claws in each other and will not loose their grip till death comes.

Then began a noise and confusion as if all the devils of hell had suddenly been let loose. We heard the shouts of the Englishmen, hoarse and deep, and the shriller cries of the Spaniards, above the roaring of the guns. On deck there sounded the wild rush and hurry of feet as the combatants were driven hither and thither. The overseers had thrown down their whips and fled to the upper decks as soon as the English boarded, and now we captives sat breathless and bleeding, listening to the noise above us and longing for release, so that we too might join in the fight.

Suddenly there leapt through one of the ports a brawny Englishman, armed not with sword or pike, but with hammer and chisel, and he was speedily followed by half-a-dozen more, armed in similar fashion.

"Are there Englishmen here?" roared the first as he tumbled in amongst us. "Speak, lads, if ye be English!"

And at that there went up such a roar as was like to burst open the deck above us. Men stretched out their hands and arms to these great English sailors as if they were angels, and prayed them to knock off their bonds. So they, staring stupidly at us for a moment, — as is the manner of Englishmen when they see something which they do not understand, — suddenly fell to and knocked away our chains and padlocks, while we wept over them and blessed them as our saviors. And meanwhile others had handed in pikes and swords and glaives through the ports, and others were guarding the ladder against the Spaniards, in case any of them should come below. But they were too busy on the upper decks to have even a thought of us, and so we were uninterrupted, and ere long every man of us was free of his chains.

"Now, lads!" cried the big man who had first leapt in upon us, "can ye fight, or are ye too weak for a brush? If any man thinks he can hold pike or sword, let him pick his weapon and follow me."

Some of us could fight and some could not. Here and there a man was only released from his chains to fall upon the deck and die. Others, suddenly made free, found on striving to rise from the benches that the use of their legs was gone. Others again, whose minds had suffered under those long months of fiendish torture, were no sooner released than they became utterly mad, and fell to laughing and gibbering at their preservers. But many of us, weak as we were, felt the strength of ten men come into our arms, and we seized eagerly upon the weapons offered to us, and followed the sailors up the gangway with a fierce resolve to call our late oppressors to a final account.

On the upper deck the fight was raging furiously. The Spaniards, furious and desperate, were massed together in a solid body, keeping back the Englishmen by sheer skill. Already between the gangways and the bulwarks lay a great heap of dead and dying. High above the combatants on the poop stood Nunez, his pale face set and drawn, watching the progress of the fight with gleaming eyes and compressed lips. From the tops the sharp-shooters were pouring showers of arrows into the English ship, but the guns had ceased, and the gunners lay dead beside them.

We dashed on deck with a great cry, and for an instant the whole body of combatants turned and looked at us. A strange and awful sight we must needs have presented at that moment. There was scarcely a rag upon us, our hair was long and unkempt, our shoulders were torn and bleeding from the effects of the lashes lately laid on them, and our entire aspect must have resembled that of wild beasts rather than of men. I saw Nunez turn paler as he caught sight of us, and heard the English storm of execration burst forth over the noise and confusion of the fight. Then we fell upon the Spaniards from behind, and after that all was red, and I seemed to do naught but strike and strike again, unconscious of pain or wounds or anything but a fierce desire to be avenged on the villains who had wrought such cruelty upon me.

Howbeit, after a time I felt myself dragged by a friendly hand out of the thick of the fight and led across the bulwarks to the English ship, where I was presently conducted on to the poop, into the presence of a man whom I at once knew to be some great captain. He was of middle height, with a high forehead, crisp brown hair, very steady gray eyes, and a hard, fierce mouth, slightly covered by a beard and moustache. He wore a loose, dark, seaman's shirt, belted at the waist, and about his neck was a plaited cord, having attached to it a ring, with which his fingers played as he spoke to me. On his head was a scarlet cap with a gold band, even as the man in the galleon had said.

Such was my first glimpse of the great captain, Francis Drake, then thirty years of age, and making his first voyage round the world. I stood staring at him for a moment, and he at me, and I know not which was most interested in the other.

"Who art thou, friend?" he inquired, presently.

"An English gentleman, sir, kidnaped by the Spaniards and carried to Mexico, where I have undergone torments at the hands of the Inquisitors. I was a galley slave on board yonder vessel."

"How many Englishmen are there with you?"

"At least forty."

"Does the ship carry treasure?"

"Yes, sir," I answered; "and she also carries two of the most cruel wretches that ever walked the earth."

"Who are they, friend?"

"Manuel Nunez, the captain, and Bartolomeo, the monk. In God's name, sir, do justice upon them."

He turned and gave some orders to an officer who stood by. Then he gave his attention to the Spanish ship again, so I caught up my weapon and rushed back over the side, eager to find Pharaoh Nanjulian.

CHAPTER XVIII.

THE FATE OF NUNEZ AND FREY BARTOLOMEO.

By that time the fight was well-nigh over. During its progress another English ship had sailed up on the other side of the Spaniard, and her men were now swarming over the side, eager to have some share in the struggle. Thus it came about that in a few moments, the Spaniards were completely worsted, and were forced to lay down their arms and beg for mercy.

I found Pharaoh Nanjulian busily occupied in seeing to the removal of several men, who were too weak to move of their own accord, from the benches where we had lately been chained. These were being carried to the English ships, where they were received with such indignation as is felt by honest men who abhor cruelty. So strong, indeed, were the feelings aroused amongst the English sailors at the sight of our bleeding backs, that their officers had much ado to prevent them from slaying the Spaniards without mercy.

"Where is the monk, Pharaoh?" I said. "He must not escape. Have you seen aught of him during the fight?"

But Pharaoh had seen naught. He had been fighting hard himself, and that being over he had turned his attention to such of our unfortunate companions as were unable to help themselves.

"He cannot be far away, master," said he. "The rat will have found some hole, no doubt."

At that moment one of Drake's officers came pressing on board, asking for the friar.

"Bring him aboard the Golden Hinde unharmed," said he, "and the Spanish captain too. 'Tis Captain Drake's special order. Harm neither of them, but have them aboard."

But neither Nunez nor Frey Bartolomeo were to be seen. Their men, such as survived — and they were but few, — stood bound on deck, glaring sullenly at their captors, but neither monk nor captain were at hand.

"Try the cabin," said one, and we made our way to the cabin under the poop, where Nunez was used to sit. But the door was fast, and we had to break it down. As the first man rushed in he fell back dead, with a sword-thrust through his heart from Nunez, while the second dropped with a dagger-wound in his throat. But ere he could strike again Pharaoh Nanjulian had seized him by the neck, and Captain Manuel Nunez was dragged into the light, dispossessed of his weapons and bound securely. I stood and looked at him, and suddenly the fierce scowl of hate and rage cleared away from his features, and the old mocking, cold smile began to play about the corners of his eyes and mouth again.

"The fortunes of war, Master Salkeld," said he. "Yesterday you were down and I was up. Today you are up and I am down. 'Tis fate."

But I had no time to talk with him then, for I was anxious to find Frey Bartolomeo. Therefore Pharaoh and I left Nunez with the officer and began searching the ship high and low. Because on first coming aboard her we had been straightway conducted to the oars we knew next to nothing of the Santa Filomena, and were accordingly some time in getting our bearings. Nevertheless we could find no trace of the monk, who seemed to have vanished into thin air, or to have gone overboard during the fight. He was not to be found either in cockpit or cabin, forecastle or lazaretto, and at last we stared blankly in each other's faces and wondered what had become of him.

"There is one place we have not yet tried," said Pharaoh, "and that is the powder magazine. Maybe he has retreated there."

We fetched a Spaniard from the upper deck and obliged him to conduct us to the magazine, and there, sure enough, was Frey Bartolomeo, calm and impassive as ever. He had stove in the head of one barrel of gunpowder, and now stood over the powder holding a lighted candle in his hand. As we burst in the door and confronted him, he raised his pale face and regarded us with calmness and scorn.

"Lay but a finger on me, ye Lutheran dogs," he said, "and I will drop this light into the powder and send your souls to perdition!"

The men with us started back, dismayed and affrighted by his grim looks and determined words. But Pharaoh Nanjulian laughed.

"Your own soul will go with ours, friar," said he.

Frey Bartolomeo shot a fierce glance at him from under his cowl.

"Fool!" he said. "Thinkest thou that I value life? What hinders me from destroying every one of you and myself as well?"

"This!" said Pharaoh, suddenly knocking the candle out of his hand. It flew across the powder, and striking a bulkhead opposite, went out harmlessly. So we seized Frey Bartolomeo, who now bitterly reproached himself for not having blown up the ship before we reached him, and conducted him to the upper deck, from whence he and Captain Nunez were presently conveyed to the Golden Hinde, where they were safely stowed in irons.

And now, the fight being over, Drake and his men made haste to see what treasure the galleon contained. In this quest, however, those of us who had been rescued from the oars took no part, for now that the excitement was dying away our feverish strength went with it, so that we presently began to exhibit signs of terrible distress and exhaustion, and many of us swooned away. Here, however, our rescuers came to our further relief, and the ship's doctor was soon busily engaged in seeing to us, dressing our wounds, giving us oils and unguents for our bloody stripes, and ordering wine and food for all of us. So we were much refreshed; but none of these things, comforting as they were, seemed so good to us as the words of kindness, which we heard with wonder and astonishment, our ears having become accustomed to naught but threatenings and revilings.

While we were occupied in this pleasant fashion, Drake's men transferred a vast amount of treasure from the Santa Filomena to the Golden Hinde. There was a large quantity of jewels, fourteen chests of ryals of plate, over a hundred pounds weight of gold, twenty tons of uncoined silver, and pieces of wrought gold and silver plate of great value. The discovery of all this treasure put our newly-found friends in high good-humor, such ventures not having come in their way since they had left the coast of Panama some months previous.

When all this treasure had been transferred to Drake's vessel, the Golden Hinde, the admiral sent for the Englishmen who had been rescued from the Santa Filomena, and gave audience to us on the quarterdeck. A sad and sorry multitude we looked, spite of the surgeon's care, as we stood gazing at the great sea-captain who had rescued us, and waiting for him to speak.

"Friends and fellow-countrymen," said he, "every one of you shall go back with me to England. We have strange tales to tell ourselves, and so, it is somewhat evident, have ye. Be content now, I will charge myself with your welfare. Where is he that spoke with me this morning?"

So I stepped forward, and he looked upon me keenly.

"Thy name, friend?"

"Humphrey Salkeld, sir, nephew of Sir Thurstan Salkeld of Beechcot, in the East Riding of Yorkshire."

"Tell me thy tale, Master Salkeld."

So I gave him the history that I have here written down, and when it came to our doings in Mexico I spoke for Pharaoh Nanjulian and for all who stood behind me. When I had got to the period which we spent on board the Santa Filomena, my companions in distress bared their shoulders and backs, and showed him the scars and the wounds and the stripes which we had received. Then his face grew stern and set and the English sailors that stood by groaned in their wrath and indignation.

"I am beholden to you, Master Salkeld," he said, when I had done. "Are there any of you that would say more?"

But none wished to speak save one old white-haired man, who lifted up his hand and called God to witness that all I had said was true, and that our torments under the Inquisition had been such as could only be prompted by the devil.

Then Drake commanded his men to bring forward Manuel Nunez and Frey Bartolomeo, and presently they stood before us, still bold and defiant, and Drake looked upon them.

"I am thinking, Senors," said he, "that if I had wrought such misdeeds upon your people as you have upon mine, and you had caught me red-handed as I have caught you, there would have been something in the way of torture for me before I came to my last end. But be not alarmed; we Englishmen love justice, but we hate cruelty. And so we will be just to you, and we will send you to your true place, where there is doubtless a reward prepared for you. Hang them to the yard-arm of their own ship."

So they carried Nunez and the monk over the side, and presently their bodies swung from the yard-arm of the Santa Filomena, and so they passed to their reward. And as for Nunez, he mocked us till the end, but the monk said never a word, but stared fixedly before him, seeming to care no more for death than he had for the sufferings that he had heaped upon his fellow-men.

After that Drake restored the Spaniards whom we had captured to their own ship, and bade them go home, or back to Mexico, or wherever they pleased, and to tell their masters what Francis Drake had done to them, and that he would do the same to every Spaniard who crossed his path.

CHAPTER XIX.

HOME WITH DRAKE.

During our awful captivity on board the galleon we had well-nigh lost all count or notion of time. To us one day was pretty much like another. If we slept it was only to be awakened by the overseer's whip. Day or night it was all one with us; never did our tormentors cease to afflict us. We were reduced to the condition of animals, and had not even the comfort which is allowed to them. Thus when the time of our rescue came, we had no notion of where we were or what part of the year it was.

We now found that it was the middle of August, and that we were in the North Pacific Ocean and bearing direct for the Moluccas, where Drake intended to trade before continuing his voyage homeward by way of the Cape. We also learnt that this great captain was now taking his first voyage round the world, and that he had had many great and remarkable adventures on the Spanish Main and on the coast of Peru, and had enriched his vessels with the spoils of Spanish treasure-ships, so that he now had with him a store of great and unusual valuc. For from some ships he had taken bars of silver, and from others blocks of gold, together with rich ladings, merchandise and silks, so rare and curious as to be worth great sums of money. And all this treasure had been chiefly won from the Spaniards in fair fight, and that without any cruelty or lust of blood or revenge.

About the thirteenth day of September we came within view of some islands, situated about eight degrees northward from the line. From these the islanders came out to us in canoes hollowed out of solid trunks of a tree, and raised very high out of the water at both ends, so that they almost formed a semicircle. These canoes were polished so highly that they shone like ebony, and were kept steady by pieces of timber fixed on each side of them by strong canes, fastened at one end to the canoe, and at the other to the timber.

The first company that came out to us brought fruits, potatoes, and other commodities, none of any great value, and seemed anxious to trade with us, making a great show of good-will and honesty. Soon after, however, they sent out another fleet of canoes, the crews of which showed themselves to be nothing better than thieves, for if we placed anything in their hands they immediately considered it to belong to them, and would neither restore nor pay for it. Upon this we were obliged to get rid of them, which we did by discharging a gun. As they had never seen ordnance discharged before they were vastly astonished by this, and fled precipitately to the shore, having first pelted us with showers of stones which they carried in their canoes.

On the fifth of November we cast anchor before Ternate, and had scarce arrived when the viceroy of that place, attended by the chief nobles, came out in three boats, rowed by forty men on each side. Soon afterwards appeared the king himself, attended by a large and imposing retinue. Him we received with discharges of cannon and musketry, together with various kinds of music, with which he was so highly delighted that he would have the musicians down into his own boat. At this place we stayed some days, trafficking with the inhabitants, who brought us large quantities of provisions, and behaved to us with civility. After that we repaired to a neighboring island, and there found a commodious harbor where we repaired the Golden Hinde, and did ourselves enjoy a much-needed rest.

Leaving this place on the 12th day of December, we sailed southwards towards the Celebes; but the wind being against us, we drifted about among a multitude of islands mingled with shallows until the middle of January. And now we met with an adventure which was like to have stayed our further progress and put a summary end to all our hopes. For sailing forward under a strong gale we were one night suddenly surprised by a shock, caused by our being thrown upon a shoal, on which the speed of our course served to fix us very fast. Upon examination we found that the rock on which we had struck rose perpendicularly from the water, and there was no anchorage, nor any bottom to be found for some distance. On making this discovery we lightened the ship by throwing into the sea a not inconsiderable portion of her lading. Even then the ship seemed hopelessly fast, and we had almost given way to despair when we were on a sudden relieved by a remission of the wind, which, having hitherto blown strongly against that side of the ship which lay towards the sea, holding it upright against the rock, now slackened, and blowing no longer against our vessel allowed it to reel into deep water, to our great comfort and relief. We had enjoyed so little hope of ever extricating ourselves from this perilous position, that Drake had caused the sacrament to be administered to us as if we had been on the point of death, and now that we were mercifully set free we sang a Te Deum and went forward very cautiously, hardly daring to set sails lest we should chance upon some reef still more dangerous.

We now continued our voyage without any remarkable occurrence or adventure, until about the middle of March we came to anchor off the Island of Java. Having sent to the king a present of clothes and silks, we received from him in return a quantity of provisions; and on the following day Drake himself went on shore, and after entertaining the king with music obtained leave from him to forage for fresh food. Here, then, we remained some days, taking in provisions, and being visited by the princes and head men of that country, and later by the king, all of whom manifested great interest in us, and in our armaments and instruments of navigation.

Leaving Java about the end of March we sailed for the Cape of Good Hope, which we sighted about the middle of June. During all that time we met with no very remarkable adventure; nevertheless, because we were sailing through seas which no Englishman had ever previously traversed there was not a day which did not present some feature of interest to us, or add to our knowledge of those strange parts of the world. To me, and to such of my companions as had suffered with me in the dungeons of the Inquisition or on the deck of the galleon, this voyage was as a glimpse of Paradise. For we were treated with the utmost kindness and consideration by Drake and his men, and they would not suffer us to undertake anything in the shape of work until our wounds were fairly healed and our strength recruited. To those of us who had suffered so bitterly that our strength was well-nigh departed, this welcome relief was very grateful. As for me, on discovering my condition I was rated with Drake and his officers, and with them did spend many exceeding pleasant hours, listening to their marvelous adventures and stories of fights with our old enemies, the Spaniards. But Pharaoh, hating to do naught, applied for a rating, and so they made him boatswain's mate, and thenceforth he was happy, and seemed quickly to forget the many privations and discomforts which he and I had undergone.

So on the third week of September, 1580, we came to Plymouth Sound, and once more looked upon English land and English faces. And this we did with such thankfulness and rejoicing as you cannot conceive. As for Drake and his men, they had been away two years and some ten months, and in that time had taken their ships round the world. And because they were the first Englishmen that had ever done this, there was such ringing of bells, and lighting of bonfires, and setting up of feasts and jollities as had never been known in England. From the queen to the meanest hind there was nobody that did not join in the general rejoicing. Wherefore, at Plymouth, where we landed, there were great stirrings, and men clung around us to hear our marvelous tales and adventures. And as for Drake himself, the queen soon afterwards made him a knight on the deck of the Golden Hinde; and so he became Sir Francis, and thereafter did many wonderful deeds which are set forth in the chronicles of that time.

Now, I no sooner set foot upon English soil than I was immediately consumed with impatience to go home to Beechcot, and therefore I sought out Drake and begged him to let me begone.

"Why," quoth he, "knowing your story as I do, Master Salkeld, I make no wonder that you should be in some haste to return to your own friends. I pray God that you may find all well with them."

Then he generously pressed upon me a sum of money in gold, wherewith to fit myself out for the journey and defray my expenses on the way; and for this kindness I was deeply grateful, seeing that I was utterly penniless, and owed the very garments I then wore to the charity of one of his officers. So I said farewell to him and his company, and begged them to remember me if we should meet no more, and then I went to find Pharaoh Nanjulian.

"Pharaoh," said I, when I came upon him on the deck of the Golden Hinde, "I am going home."

He pushed back his cap and scratched his head and looked at me.

"Aye," he said, "I supposed it would be so, master. As for me, I have no home to go to. My mother is dead and buried in Marazion churchyard, and I have neither kith nor kin in the wide world."

"Come with me to Beechcot," said I, "you shall abide there for the rest of your days in peace and plenty."

But he shook his head.

"Nay, master," he answered, "that would never do. I am naught but a rough sea-dog, and I should be too big and savage for a quiet life. Besides, yon constable of yours would be forever at my heels, fearing lest I should break the peace again."

"There shall no man harm you if you will come with me," said I. "Come and be my man."

"Nay, master, not so. Born and bred to the sea I was, and to the sea I will cleave. Besides, I am Francis Drake's man now, and with him I shall see rare ventures. Already there is talk of an expedition against the Spaniards. That is the life for me."

So there was no more to be said, and I gave him my hand sorrowfully, for he had proved a true friend.

"Good-bye, then, Pharaoh Nanjulian."

"Good-bye, master. We have seen some rare ventures together. I thank God for bringing us safely out of them."

"Amen! I shall not forget them or thee. And God grant we may meet again."

So we pressed each other's hands with full hearts, and I went away and left him gazing after me.

CHAPTER XX.

BEECHCOT ONCE MORE.

Because it was autumn, I found some slight difficulty in traveling across country from Plymouth to Beechcot, and it accordingly was several days before I reached York and entered upon the final stage of my journey. At Plymouth I had bought a stout horse, and pushed forward, mounted in creditable fashion, to Exeter, and from thence to Bristol, where I struck into the Midlands and made for Derby and Sheffield. It took me a fortnight to reach York, and there, my horse being well-nigh spent, though I had used him with mercy, I exchanged him for a cob, which was of stout build, and good enough to carry me over the thirty miles which yet remained of my journey.

Now, as I drew near the old place, in the twilight of a dull October afternoon, my heart beat within my breast as if it would suffocate me. I had been away two years, and had gone under circumstances of the strangest character. Those whom I had left behind had probably long since given me up as dead. Worse than that — how did I know what malicious story might not have been invented and set forth by my cousin Jasper as to my disappearance? Well, the time was now at hand when all should be explained. But yet — what changes might there not be? I dreaded to think of them. I might find my good uncle dead, Jasper in possession, my sweetheart married — but nay, that seemed hardly to be believed. And yet if she thought me dead?

Thus I went forward, my heart torn by many conflicting emotions. Then I began to think of the changes that had taken place in me. Two years ago I had set out a light-hearted, careless lad, full of confidence and ignorance, knowing naught of the world nor of its cruelties. Now I came back a man, full of strange experiences, my mind charged with many terrible memories, my body bearing witness of the sufferings and privations which I had undergone. It was not the old Humphrey Salkeld that rode down Beechcot village street. Nay, it was not even the old Humphrey Salkeld in looks. Stopping a few hours at the inn in York I had examined myself in a mirror, and had decided that it would be hard work for my old friends to recognize me. I had grown an inch or two, my face was seamed and wrinkled, and wore a strange, grim, wearied look, my beard was a good three inches long, and my mouth covered by a moustache. Changed I was indeed.

I rode up to the door of the inn at Beechcot, where I had first seen Pharaoh Nanjulian, and called loudly for the host. There was no one about the door of the inn, but presently Geoffrey Scales, looking no different to what he did when I had last seen him, came bustling along the sanded passage with his lantern, and turned the light full on my face. I trembled, and could scarce control my voice as I spoke to him; but I soon saw that he did not recognize me.

"How far is it to Scarborough, master?" I inquired.

"A good twenty miles, sir, and a bad road."

"What, are there thieves on it?"

"There are highwaymen, sir, and ruts, which is worse; and as for mud — there, your honor would be lost in it."

"Then I had better stay here for the night, eh?"

"Much better, if your honor pleases."

So I dismounted and bade him take my cob round to his stable, and followed him myself to hear more news.

"What place is this?" I inquired.

"Beechcot, sir — a village of the Wolds."

"And who owns it, landlord?"

"Sir Thurstan Salkeld, sir."

"Is he alive and well, landlord?"

Now, whether it was my voice or the unwonted agitation in it that attracted his attention, I know not, but certain it is that when I asked this question Geoffrey Scales held up his light to my face, and after anxiously peering therein for a moment, cried out loudly:

"Marry, I knew it! 'Tis Master Humphrey, come home again, alive and well!" and therewith he would have rushed away to rouse the whole village if I had not stayed him.

"Hush! Geoffrey," I said. "It is I, true enough, and I am well enough, but prithee keep quiet awhile, for I do not wish anyone to know that I have returned for a season. Tell me first how is my uncle and Mistress Rose. Are they well, Geoffrey? Quick!"

"Oh, Master Humphrey," quoth he, "what a turn you have given me! Yes, sir, yes; your uncle, good man, is well, though he hath never been the same man since you disappeared, Master Humphrey. And as for Mistress Rose, 'tis just the same sweet maiden as ever, and hath grieved for you mightily. But what a to-do there will be, Master Humphrey! Prithee, let me go and tell all the folk."

"Not now, Geoffrey, on thy life. Let me first see my sweetheart and my uncle, and then I will cause the great bell at the manor to be rung, and you shall take it for a signal and shall tell who you like."

So he promised to obey me, and I left him and took my way towards the vicarage, for my heart longed sore for the presence of my sweetheart.

Now, as I came up to the front of the house there was a light burning in the parlor, and I stole up to the window and looked in, and saw Rose busy with her needle. Fair and sweet she was, aye, sweeter, I think, than ever; but it was easy to see that she had sorrowed, and that the sorrow had left its mark upon her. I had always remembered her in my trials and torments as the merry, laughing maiden, that had flown hither and thither like a spirit of spring; now I saw her a woman, sweet and lovely, but with a touch of sadness about her that I knew had come there because of me.

I went round to the door and tapped softly upon it. Presently came Rose, bearing a candle, and opened it to my knock, and looked out upon me. I drew farther away into the darkness.

"Is this the abode of Master Timotheus Herrick?" I asked.

"Yes, sir," she answered, "but he is not in at this moment. You will find him at the church, where he has gone to read the evening service."

"I had a message for his daughter," said I.

"I am his daughter, sir. What message have you for me?"

"I have come from sea," I answered. "It is a message from one you know."

"From one I know — at sea? But I know no one at sea. Oh, sir, what is it you would tell me?"

"Let me come in," I said; and she turned and led the way into the parlor, and set down the candle and looked steadily at me. And then she suddenly knew me, and in another instant I had her in my arms, and her face was upon my breast, and all the woes and sorrows of my captivity were forgotten.

"Humphrey!" she cried. "O, thank God — thank God! My dear, my dear, it is you, is it not? Am I dreaming — shall I wake presently to find you gone?"

"Never again, sweetheart, never again! I am come back indeed — somewhat changed, it is true, but still your true and faithful lover."

"And I thought you were dead! O my poor Humphrey, where have you been and what has been done to you? Yes, you are changed — you have suffered, have you not?"

"More than I could wish my worst enemy to suffer," I answered. "But I forget it all when I look at you, Rose. Oh, sweetheart, if you knew how I have longed for this moment!"

And then, hand in hand, we kneeled down together and thanked God for all his goodness, and for the marvelous mercy with which he had brought us through this time of sore trouble. And on our knees we kissed each other solemnly, and so sealed our reunion, and blotted out all the bitterness of the past from our hearts, so that there was nothing left there but memories, sad indeed, but no longer painful.

"And now," said Rose, "tell me, Humphrey, where you have been and how it was you went away. Oh, if you knew how we have sorrowed for you."

"First tell me, Rose, how is my uncle?"

"He is well, Humphrey, but he has mourned for you ever since Jasper came home and told us of your death."

"Ah! Jasper came home and told you of my death, did he? And by what manner of death did I die, according to Master Jasper?"

"He said you were drowned at Scarborough, in coming from some vessel where you and he had been paying a visit at night to the captain."

"And did no one doubt him, Rose? Were there no inquiries made?"

"I doubted him, Humphrey. I felt sure there was some strange mystery, but how could I find it out? And what could be done — they could not drag Scarborough Bay for your body. Humphrey, did Jasper play some trick upon you — did he get you out of the way?"

"He did, Rose. Yea, he got me out of the way so well that I have been right round the world since last I set foot in Beechcot. Think of that, my dear. Right round the world! I have seen Mexico and the Pacific and Java and the Celebes and Africa, and I know not what, and here I am again."

"But you have suffered, Humphrey? Where — and how?"

So I told her very briefly of what had happened to me in the cells of the Inquisition, and as I spoke, her sweet face was filled with compassion and her eyes were bright with tears, and she held my hands tightly clasped in her own as if she would never let them go again.

"Can such things be?" she asked. "Oh, why God does allow them I cannot understand. My poor Humphrey!"

"Naught but God's help could have brought us through them, dear heart," I answered. "And, indeed, I think naught of them now, and would cheerfully face them again if I thought they would cause you to love me more."

But she answered that that was impossible, and scolded me very prettily for thinking of such a thing.

And then came Master Timotheus back from reading prayers, and entered the parlor, carrying a great folio in his hand and blinking at us through his big spectacles. And when he saw me, he stopped and stared.

"Here is a visitor, father," said Rose. "Look closely at him — do you not know him?"

But the good man, taking my hand in his own, did stare at me hard and long ere he discovered me, and then he fell upon my neck and embraced me heartily and wept with joy.

"Of a truth," said he, "I might have known that it was thee, Humphrey, for two reasons. First, I have been of an uncommonly light-hearted nature all this day, and did once detect myself in the act of singing a merry song; and secondly, I saw on entering the parlor that Rose's face was brighter than it hath been since last we saw thee."

Then he laid his hand on my head and blessed me, and thanked God for sending me home again; and he shed more tears, and was fain to take off his spectacles and polish them anew. And he would have had me sup with them, but on hearing that I had not yet seen my uncle he bade me go to him at once, so I said farewell for that time and took my way to the manor.

CHAPTER XXI.

HOW THEY RANG THE BELLS AT BEECHCOT CHURCH

As I walked across from the vicarage to the manor house, the moon came out in the autumn evening sky and lighted the landscape with a brightness that was little short of daylight. I stood for a few moments at the vicarage gate admiring the prospect. Far away to the eastward rose the Wolds, dark and unbroken, different indeed from the giant bulk of Orizaba, but far more beautiful to me. Beneath them lay the village of Beechcot, with its farmsteads and cottages casting black shadows upon the moonlit meadow, and here and there a rushlight burning dimly in the windows. I had kept that scene in my mind's eye many a time during my recent tribulations, and had wondered if ever I should see it again. Now that I did see it, it was far more beautiful than I had ever known it or imagined it to be, for it meant home, and love, and peace after much sorrow.

My path led me through the churchyard. There the moonlight fell bright and clear on the silent mounds and ghostly tombstones. By thc chancel I paused for a moment to glance at the monument which Sir Thurstan had long since erected to my father and mother's memory. It was light enough to read the inscription, and also to see that a new one had been added to it. Wondering what member of our family was dead, I went nearer and examined the stone more carefully. Then I saw that the new inscription was in memory of myself!

I have never heard of a man reading his own epitaph, and truly it gave me many curious feelings to stand there and read of myself as a dead man. And yet I had been dead to all of them for more than two years.

"And of Humphrey Salkeld, only son of the above Richard Salkeld and his wife Barbara, who was drowned at Scarborough, October, 1578, to the great grief and sorrow of his uncle, Thurstan Salkeld, Knight."

"So I am dead and yet alive," I said, and laughed gayly at the notion. "If that is so, there are some great surprises in store for more than one in this parish. And no one will be more surprised than my worthy cousin, but he will be the only person that is sorry to see me. Oh, for half an hour with him alone!"

At that very moment Jasper was coming to meet me. I knew it not, nor did he.

Between the churchyard and the manor-house of Beechcot there is a field called the Duke's Garth, and across this runs a foot-path. As I turned away from reading my own epitaph, I saw a figure advancing along this path and making for the churchyard. It was the figure of a man, and he was singing some catch or song softly to himself. I recognized the voice at once. It was Jasper's. I drew back into the shadow cast by the buttress of the chancel and waited his coming. We were going to settle our account once and forever.

He came lightly over the stile which separates the garth from the churchyard, and was making rapid strides towards the vicarage when I stopped him.

"Jasper," I said, speaking in a deep voice and concealing myself in the shadow. "Jasper Stapleton."

He stopped instantly, and stood looking intently towards where I stood.

"Who calls me?" he said.

"I, Jasper, — thy cousin, Humphrey Salkeld."

I could have sworn that he started and began to tremble. But suddenly he laughed.

"Dead men call nobody," said he. "You are some fool that is trying to frighten me. Come out, sirrah!"

And he drew near. I waited till he was close by, and then I stepped into the moonlight, which fell full and clear on my face. He gave a great cry, and lifting up his arm as if to ward off a blow fell back a pace or two and stood staring at me.

"Humphrey!" he cried.

"None other, cousin. The dead, you see, sometimes come to life again. And I am very much alive, Jasper."

He stood still staring at me, and clutching his heart as if his breath came with difficulty.

"What have you to say, Jasper?" I asked at length.

"We — we thought you were drowned," he gasped out. "There is an inscription on your father's tombstone."

"Liar!" I said. "You know I was not drowned. You know that you contrived that I should be carried to Mexico. Tell me no more lies, cousin. Let us for once have the plain truth. Why did you treat me as you did at Scarborough?"

"Because you stood 'twixt me and the inheritance," he muttered sullenly.

"And so for the sake of a few acres of land and a goodly heritage you would condemn one who had never harmed you to horrors such as you cannot imagine?" I said. "Look at me, Jasper. Even in this light it is not difficult to see how I am changed. I have gone through such woes and torments as you would scarcely credit. I have been in the hands of devils in human shape, and they have so worked their will upon me that there is hardly an inch of my body that is not marked and scarred. That was thy doing, Jasper, — thine and thy fellow-villain's. Dost know what happened to him?"

"No," he whispered, "what of him?"

"I saw him hanged to his own yard-arm in the Pacific Ocean, Jasper, and he went to his own place with the lives of many an innocent man upon his black soul. Take care you do not follow him. Shame upon you, cousin, for the trick you played me!"

"You came between me and the girl I loved," he said fiercely. "All is fair in love and war."

"Coward!" I said. "And liar, too! I never came between her and thee, for she had never a word to give such a black-hearted villain as thou hast proved thyself. And now, what is to prevent me from taking my revenge upon thee, Jasper?"

"This," he said, very suddenly, whipping out his rapier. "This, Master Humphrey. Home you have come again, worse luck, and have no doubt done your best to injure me in more quarters than one, but you shall not live to enjoy either land, or title, or sweetheart, for you shall die here and now."

And with that he came pressing upon me with a sudden fury that was full of murderous intent.

Now I had no weapon by me save a stout cudgel which I had cut from a coppice by the wayside that morning, and this you would think was naught when set against a rapier. Nevertheless I made such play with it, that presently I knocked Jasper's weapon clean out of his hand so that he could not recover it. And after that I seized him by the throat and beat with my cudgel until he roared and begged for mercy, beseeching me not to kill him.

"Have no fear, cousin," said I, still laying on to him, "I will not kill thee, for I would have thee repent of all thy misdeeds."

And with that I gave him two or three sound cuts and then flung him from me against the wall, where he lay groaning and cursing me.

After that I saw Jasper Stapleton no more. He never showed his face in Beechcot again, and in a few days his mother, Dame Barbara, disappeared also; and so they vanished out of my life, and I was glad of it, for they had worked me much mischief.

When I reached the manor-house I let myself in by a secret way that I knew of and went straight to the great hall, where sat my uncle, Sir Thurstan, wrapped in cloaks and rugs, before a great fire of wood. He was all alone, and hearing my step he half turned his head.

"Is that Jasper?" he inquired.

"Nay, sir," said I. "It is I — Humphrey — and I am come home again."

And I went forward and kneeled down before him and put my hands on his knees.

For a moment he stared at me as men stare at ghosts, then he gave a great sob of delight, stretched out his arms, put them about my neck, and wept over me like a woman.

"Oh lad, lad!" said he. "If thou didst but know how this old heart did grieve for thy sake. And thou art here, well and strong, and I did cause thy name to be graven on thy parents' tombstone!"

"Never mind, sir," said I, "we can cut it out again. Anyway I am not dead, but I have seen some rare and terrible adventures."

"Sit thyself down at my side," quoth he, "and tell me all about them. Alive and well — yes, and two inches taller, as I live! Well, I thank God humbly. But thou art hungry, poor boy, — what ho! where are those rascals? Call for them, Humphrey, — thou must be famished."

"All in good time, sir," said I, and went over to the rope which led to the great bell and pulled it vigorously, so that the clangor filled the park below with stirring sound. And Geoffrey Scales, waiting impatiently at the inn, heard it and ran round with the news, and they rang the church bells, and every soul in Beechcot that could walk came hurrying to the manor and would have audience of me in the great hall.

Thus did I come home again. And having told my story to my uncle, Sir Thurstan, and to Master Timotheus Herrick, we agreed that for the present we would leave Jasper Stapleton's name out of it. But somehow, most likely because Jasper and his evil-tongued mother disappeared, the truth got out, and ere long everybody knew my story from beginning to end.

Within a few weeks of my home-coming Rose and I were married in Beechcot church, and again the bells rang out merrily. Never had bridegroom a sweeter bride; never had husband a truer or nobler wife. I say it after fifty years of blessed companionship, and in my heart I thank God for the delights which he hath given me in her.

And now I have brought my history to a close. Yet there is one matter which I must speak of before I say farewell to you.

It is about twenty years since one of my servants came to me one summer evening and said that an old man stood at my door waiting to see me. I followed him presently, and there saw a tall, white-haired, white-bearded figure, dressed in a rough seaman's dress and leaning upon a staff. He looked at me and smiled, and then I saw that it was Pharaoh Nanjulian.

"You have not forgotten me, master?" he said.

"Forgotten thee! May God forget me if ever I forget thee, my old, true friend!" I said, and I led him in and made him welcome as a king to my house and to all that I had. And with me he lived, an honored guest and friend, for ten years longer, when he died, being then a very old man of near one hundred years. And him I still mourn with true sorrow and affection, for his was a mighty heart, and it had been knit to mine by those bonds of sorrow which are scarcely less strong than the bonds of love.

THE END

Made in the USA
Columbia, SC
23 August 2023

21982743R00086